NEW DIRECTIONS FOR TEACHING AND LEARNING

Robert J. Menges, *Northwestern University*
EDITOR-IN-CHIEF

Marilla D. Svinicki, *University of Texas, Austin*
ASSOCIATE EDITOR

Ethical Dimensions of College and University Teaching: Understanding and Honoring the Special Relationship Between Teachers and Students

Linc. Fisch
EDITOR

Number 66, Summer 1996

JOSSEY-BASS PUBLISHERS
San Francisco

ETHICAL DIMENSIONS OF COLLEGE AND UNIVERSITY TEACHING:
UNDERSTANDING AND HONORING THE SPECIAL RELATIONSHIP
BETWEEN TEACHERS AND STUDENTS
Linc. Fisch (ed.)
New Directions for Teaching and Learning, no. 66
Robert J. Menges, Editor-in-Chief
Marilla D. Svinicki, Associate Editor

Microfilm copies of issues and articles are available in 16mm and 35mm,
as well as microfiche in 105mm, through University Microfilms Inc., 300
North Zeeb Road, Ann Arbor, Michigan 48106-1346.

ISSN 0271-0633   ISBN 0-7879-9910-5

NEW DIRECTIONS FOR TEACHING AND LEARNING is part of The Jossey-Bass
Higher and Adult Education Series and is published quarterly by Jossey-
Bass Inc., Publishers, 350 Sansome Street, San Francisco, California
94104-1342. Second-class postage paid at San Francisco, California, and
at additional mailing offices. POSTMASTER: Send address changes to New
Directions for Teaching and Learning, Jossey-Bass Inc., Publishers, 350
Sansome Street, San Francisco, California 94104-1342.

SUBSCRIPTIONS for 1996 cost $50.00 for individuals and $72.00 for institutions, agencies, and libraries.

EDITORIAL CORRESPONDENCE should be sent to the editor-in-chief, Robert J.
Menges, Northwestern University, Center for the Teaching Professions,
2115 North Campus Drive, Evanston, Illinois 60208-2610.

Academic principles of responsibility in Chapter Nine reprinted from *Ethics
in Higher Education*, edited by William W. May. Used by permission of the
Council on American Education and Oryx Press, 4041 No. Central Ave.,
Phoenix, AZ 85012. 800/279-6799.

Chapter Thirteen epigraph is from "Putting It Together," music and lyrics
by Stephen Sondheim © 1984 Rilting Music Inc. All rights administered
by WB Music Corp. All rights reserved. Used by permission. Warner Bros.
Publications U.S. Inc., Miami, FL 33014.

Cover photograph by Richard Blair/Color & Light © 1990.

TCF Manufactured in the United States of America on Lyons Falls
Pathfinder Tradebook. This paper is acid-free and 100 percent
totally chlorine-free.

Contents

FROM THE SERIES EDITORS

About This Publication. Since 1980, *New Directions for Teaching and Learning (NDTL)* has brought a unique blend of theory, research, and practice to leaders in postsecondary education. *NDTL* sourcebooks strive not only for solid substance but also for timeliness, compactness, and accessibility.

The series has four goals: to inform readers about current and future directions in teaching and learning in postsecondary education, to illuminate the context that shapes these new directions, to illustrate these new directions through examples from real settings, and to propose ways in which these new directions can be incorporated into still other settings.

This publication reflects our view that teaching deserves respect as a high form of scholarship. We believe that significant scholarship is conducted not only by researchers who report results of empirical investigations but also by practitioners who share disciplined reflections about teaching. Contributors to *NDTL* approach questions of teaching and learning as seriously as they approach substantive questions in their own disciplines, and they deal not only with pedagogical issues but also with the intellectual and social context in which these issues arise. Authors deal on the one hand with theory and research and on the other with practice, and they translate from research and theory to practice and back again.

About This Volume. This issue of *New Directions for Teaching and Learning* includes several perspectives on the ethical dimensions of teaching and learning. Chapter authors analyze conceptual and philosophical issues, examine particularly problematic situations such as grading and evaluation, and offer guidelines and principles intended to inform decisions about ethical matters. Each chapter illuminates the professor's obligation to be consistently fair and respectful in dealing with students, colleagues, and others, while at the same time maintaining a sense of personal integrity. All in all, these chapters constitute an array of provocative resources for contemplation and discussion by members of the academic community.

Robert J. Menges, *Editor-in-Chief*
Marilla D. Svinicki, *Associate Editor*

EDITOR'S NOTES

The watchword of our times is accountability, and teachers in colleges and universities have not escaped close scrutiny by the public, press, and politicians. Instances of general misconduct and ethical laxity do occur, and some of them garner prominence through media attention. But those cases are relatively few, and there seems to be little reason to suppose that unethical behavior runs rampant within the professoriate. Then is all well in academia? Whatever the answer, those who judge our profession, as those who score ice-skating competition, always see room at the top for improvement.

To be sure, it is important for faculty members to meet explicit and implicit contractual obligations and to avoid public criticism and legal sanction. Fulfilling one's responsibilities through complying with standards is a minimal ethic, one surely to be insisted upon, as Audi (1994) points out. But there is a force of higher order that drives professors to be ethical. We should strive, Audi adds, for the professional ethics worthy of our aspiration—those ideals that arise from the relationship between teacher and student. The predominant impetus toward teaching ethically is the nature of that special relationship in which both participants are transformed to elevated levels of thought, standards, and performance.

I think it likely that most faculty members are generally aware of the broad ethical rules—even the ideals—that pertain to the academic endeavor. Beyond knowledge, it is *commitment* to those rules and ideals that is necessary for an ethical professoriate. And if teachers are to be *fully* prepared to reduce the incidence of ethical problems—and to resolve them satisfactorily when they occur—they need to develop an ever deeper awareness of the subtleties of application of ethical principles and an understanding of the gray areas between what is ethical and what is not ethical. There also is relevance to a pedagogical imperative: by giving visible attention to teaching ethically, faculty members model and advocate ethical behavior to students, thereby teaching in a voice more effective than any proclamation, however loud and bold. And no matter how ethically teachers already function, there is always room at the top for even higher performance.

Ethical issues pervade all aspects of college and university life. By design, this volume focuses almost exclusively on the ethical dimensions of *teaching*, rather than of research and other academic responsibilities of professors. The authors of these chapters bring fresh insights and perspectives to these dimensions, which they hope will inform and enrich discussions among faculty members, administrators, and all who have contact with students. They further hope that such efforts will enhance the level of ethical behavior in this noble enterprise called teaching.

In the opening chapter, David C. Smith provides us with philosophical background, basing his discussion of the teacher-student relationship on Martin

Buber's I–Thou relationship. The nature of our work demands that we reflect on our craft as an ethical endeavor (Smith borrows the term from Alan Tom and builds upon Tom's able defense of such a characterization). That reflection, Smith says, thereby becomes a source of self-renewal and, ideally, of public renewal. In Chapter Two, Mary Burgan turns our attention to students' developmental stages as an important consideration in teaching ethically. We become a part of the developmental process and thereby ourselves become transformed along with our students.

The next three chapters examine specific aspects of ethical behavior in teaching. Richard Baker uses May Sarton's novel *The Small Room* as a case study to discover successful and unsuccessful instances of faculty members' becoming friends with students. He suggests "mediated intimacy" as a necessary condition for friendships with students to be salutary. In Chapter Four, Karen Hanson discusses situations where courses include issues about which teachers (and students) feel strongly. Rejecting both partisan persuasion and apathy toward issues, she recommends that teaching should be governed by the virtues of openness, honesty, courtesy, and civil respect, thus modeling ethical behavior for students. In Chapter Five, Rita Rodabaugh examines fairness, perhaps the most common ethical issue in higher education, and she details what may be done to ensure commitment to fairness throughout an institution.

In Chapter Six, Terry Ray takes a critical look at ethics, morality, law, and justice. Unless we differentiate among the meanings of these related concepts, he says, we are doomed to circular disputation and unproductive deliberations on ethical issues.

The authors of the next three chapters offer sets of principles and responsibilities that they regard as comprehensive lists of standards for ethical behavior. Clark Kerr lists fifteen components in his "ethics of knowledge," many of which pertain to teaching. Harry Murray and his colleagues have developed nine "ethical principles in university teaching," along with examples that illustrate and clarify their application. Charles Reynolds poses twenty-seven "academic principles of responsibility," organized into five categories: personal, professional, systemic, public, and political. He also offers a process for making responsible ethical decisions.

In Chapter Ten, Patricia Keith-Spiegel and her associates offer suggestions for action, should one encounter ethical transgressions by a colleague. In Chapter Eleven, Ronald Smith presents a rationale and a process that individual faculty members may employ in reflecting upon the ethics of their own behavior. In the penultimate chapter, I list a number of additional resources on the ethical dimensions of teaching and suggest how colleges and universities can undertake workshops and initiate other activities that could help enhance the climate for ethical teaching.

In the final chapter, Kathleen McGrory reflects on the previous chapters. In searching for themes, she finds that there emerges a dominant principle: responsibility to students is directly related to understanding of one's ethical self. Further, the first step in establishing that ethical identity is self-reflection.

Ethical teaching requires transformations of structures and attitudes and persons—faculty as well as students—if the promise of American higher education is to be realized. That is the clear, collective message of the contributors to this sourcebook.

Carter (1996) reinforces the theme that integrity requires reflection leading toward discernment of what is right and what is wrong. But that is not a sufficient condition for integrity, he says; we must also act upon what we come to believe and then take a critical third step of being open and public about our beliefs and actions. Only thus can we fully meet with integrity our responsibilities to ourselves and our students—and to our society.

Please permit me a few personal notes. I thank Patricia Keith-Spiegel, Ralph Lundgren, Wilbert J. McKeachie, Kathleen McGrory, Brian Schrag, and David H. Smith for their support and valuable advice during the early stages of this project. I am especially grateful to the chapter authors who gave so willingly and freely of time, thought, experience, and effort in order to bring to fruition an endeavor dear to the hearts of all of us. And allow me also to recognize the late Algo Henderson, whose spirit, integrity, and quiet influence helped guide my way for many years.

References

Audi, R. "On the Ethics of Teaching and the Ideals of Learning." *Academe,* 1994, *80* (5), 27–36.

Carter, S. L. *Integrity.* New York: Basic Books, 1996.

Linc. Fisch
Editor

LINC. FISCH *held teaching appointments (mathematics, college teaching, community dentistry, and public health) as well as administrative and program development assignments in several colleges and universities in Ohio, Michigan, and Kentucky for more than thirty-five years. He lives in Lexington, Kentucky, and is actively retired.*

The ethical bond between teachers and students is considered as a form of the I–Thou relationship as articulated by Martin Buber. This bond raises the issues of fairness, honesty, promise-keeping, respect, and responsibility as norms for teachers.

The Ethics of Teaching

David C. Smith

In the *Protagoras*, Socrates is awakened before dawn by his young friend Hippocrates, who wants to rush at this impossible hour to the house where the visiting sophist Protagoras is staying so that he can engage Protagoras as a teacher. Socrates urges calm upon Hippocrates and begins his usual custom of asking questions. At first the answers seem obvious to the young man, but he is soon left in perplexity. Why, asks Socrates, is he so eager to pay his tuition to Protagoras? If Hippocrates were going to pay a physician or a sculptor for instruction, the object would be clear—to learn the techniques of a physician or a sculptor. But what does Hippocrates expect to become by paying Protagoras? Wise, Hippocrates ventures. Wise *about what?* As Hippocrates becomes confused, Socrates admonishes him for not perceiving what is ultimately at stake in his choice of a teacher—stakes that are involved in the choice of any teacher who aspires to more than merely conveying technical information or demonstrating technique (Plato, 1956 ed., p. 43):

> Well then . . . do you realize the sort of danger to which you are going to expose your soul? If it were a case of putting your body into the hands of someone and risking the treatment turning out beneficial or the reverse, you would ponder deeply whether to entrust it to him or not, and would spend many days over the question, calling on the counsel of your friends and relations; but when it comes to something which you value more highly than your body, namely your soul—something on whose beneficial or harmful treatment your whole welfare depends—you have not consulted either your father or your brother or any of us who are your friends on the question of whether or not to entrust your soul to this stranger who has arrived among us.

While I have little to say by way of agreement with Allan Bloom, I think that part of the commercial success of *The Closing of the American Mind* (1987) is attributable to the fact that he recaptures Socrates' sense of souls-in-peril in his subtitle: *How Higher Education Has Failed Democracy and Impoverished the Souls of Today's Students*. For our explorations, too, we are indebted to Socrates if this metaphor of souls-at-stake gives a sense of urgency to our reflections about the ethical responsibilities of teachers. Amidst the complexities of our profession and with our postmodern awareness of the fragmentary and fluid nature of human identity, even those of us who readily acknowledge the moral purposes of education may need occasional renewal of the imagination that prompts us to consider the deep consequences of our actions and thus of the responsibilities that are ours.

This chapter consists of three major sections. In the first, I consider the nature of the relationship between teacher and student to elicit the special kind of responsibility that comes to us in our role as teachers. Second, there are a number of specific, day-to-day ethical issues involved in this relationship, and I want to raise and comment on several of those issues. Finally, I shall return to the concept of responsibility and suggest some of the ways in which we may occasionally have ethical obligations to students that extend beyond our role of responsibility in the narrower sense of our responsibilities as teachers.

Concepts of the Student-Teacher Relationship

My understanding of the student-teacher relationship has been informed principally by the writings of Alan Tom, James MacGregor Burns, and Martin Buber. It will be useful to briefly review their perspectives before delineating the special responsibilities that the relationship elicits.

Tom's Three Models of the Relationship. In his book *Teaching as a Moral Craft,* Alan Tom sketches three models of the teacher-student relationship that help us begin to think about our ethical responsibilities as teachers. The models share a general conception of teaching as "intentional activity designed to bring about student learning" (1984, p. 81) and a recognition of the institutional context of the teacher-student relationship. Beyond that, they differ in regard to their understandings of the goal of teaching. The various goals proposed lead to differing sets of ethical obligations for the three models.

The first model focuses on the teacher as *transmitter and interpreter of socially-useful knowledge.* The heart of the teacher's moral obligation is taking responsibility for the development of the student, and the student's responsibility is to master the knowledge and skills conveyed and to respect the authority of the teacher. I admit that this model is often conservative and paternalistic. At its worst, it seems to assume that learning is a passive process of acquiring information, but this need not be the case. Active learning can surely be included among the skills that teachers have and that students are expected to master.

Moreover, I think the model assumes that the teacher is passing on not merely facts but also the social and professional *values* that undergird a discipline or profession. We can convey to students our own experiences as active learners as we think through texts or problems in the classroom. We can ask them to master and demonstrate these skills in the same context. Even my former colleague who professed that his *only* goal as a teacher was "to turn out little physicists" surely had more in mind than just transmitting information. He was concerned about the development of students, albeit their development in his own image.

The transmission model also has the courage to confront the educational inequality of teacher and student, rather than seeking to avoid the discomfort we often feel in dealing with inequality. The key ethical obligation of the teacher is to take responsibility for interpreting and conveying ideas and skills, in a context of intellectual inequality, to students who lack the knowledge and skills in question. This obligation includes setting forth standards for the attribution and the presentation of data to those who are not fully positioned to appreciate those standards. Legitimate authority over students accompanies the intellectual authority of the teacher.

The second model for the teacher-student relationship derives from the *moral equality of teachers and students.* This model focuses on the obligations of fairness and respect for persons that follow from that moral equality. In the second part of this chapter, I will examine a number of issues to which these general criteria of fairness and respect for persons must be applied. Here I merely note how the shift from the intellectual dimension to the moral dimension of the teacher-student relationship moves us from considerations of obligations under conditions of inequality to obligations under conditions of equality. I think that most instances of unethical conduct by teachers arise under one of the three following conditions: the two dimensions of the relationship are confused; one dimension is subordinated to the other; or the two aspects are artificially considered in total separation, rather than being recognized as both parts of a complex—I would say unique—interpersonal relationship.

Let me give two brief examples of the considerations that arise when the moral equality model is applied. First of all, equality implies *reciprocity.* We must not do things to our students that would offend our own sense of moral worth. This might prompt us to ask ourselves questions of this sort: do we interrupt students when they are speaking? Do we give reasons for our judgments of their work? Do we make comments (intentional or not) that destroy their sense of self-worth?

Second, equality demands *fairness.* If the highly personal nature of the teacher-student relationship means that we cannot treat all students in exactly the same way, what efforts do we make to be certain that we are treating students equitably? What steps do we take to be sure that we do not play favorites? I shall return to a more detailed consideration of fairness issues later.

Alan Tom's third model of the teacher-student relationship is based on Paulo Freire's concept of *problem-posing teaching.* Here, says Tom (1984, p. 85), "the entire question of teacher authority becomes irrelevant and even the separation between teacher and student tends to dissolve." The subject matter at hand is not the "private property" of the teacher, but "the object of reflection by himself and the students," who are "co-investigators in dialogue with the teacher." The teacher (Freire, in Tom, 1984, p. 86) "presents the material to the students for their consideration, and re-considers his earlier considerations as the students express their own."

This third model has clear roots in a philosophy of human liberation and is open, of course, to radically egalitarian interpretations of roles and authority. But I find the model helpful even within my own moderate liberal-reformist perspective. First, the model assumes the shared ownership of knowledge, and places responsibility for active learning more forcefully on students than does the transmission model (in which the imperative to learn comes forth as a somewhat abstract social duty). Above all, Freire (in Tom, 1984, pp. 85ff) seems to capture a more active dialectic of teaching and learning that expresses, more or less, the way in which many of us actually do learn from our students when things are going right in the classroom. "The teacher-of-the-students and the students-of-the-teacher cease to exist and a new term emerges: teacher-student with students-teachers. The teacher is no longer merely the one-who-teaches, but one who is himself taught in dialogue with the students, who in turn while being taught also teach."

A few campuses have attempted to institutionalize the role of faculty members as "master learners" in "learning communities." On many campuses, interdisciplinary courses and team teaching serve as structured opportunities for faculty members to present themselves as learners. This routinely happens when students and teachers are both genuinely engaged with a problem or a text.

Burns's Transactional and Transforming Relationships. In his award-winning book, *Leadership* (1978), James MacGregor Burns makes the distinction between *transactional* and *transforming* leadership. Although I will sketch briefly what Burns means by each term, the gist of the distinction is fairly obvious. It is also helpful in getting at the ideal of the teacher-student relationship and thus at the deepest moral potential of this relationship.

In *transactional* relationships, says Burns, the leader and followers are involved in an exchange of valued things. As applied to the teacher-student relationship, we might understand the transaction to be that students pay their tuition and invest their time and effort in order to get things that they expect— in this case, knowledge, expertise, grades, and credentials.

Even at the transactional level, the relationship of the parties is subtle and complex. Burns (1978, pp. 19ff) writes, "Each party to the bargain is conscious of the power resources and attitudes of the other. Each person recognizes the other as a *person*. Their purposes are related, at least to the extent that the purposes stand within the bargaining process and can be advanced by maintaining that process."

A lot of what we do as teachers seems to fit Burns's model of transactional leadership. We take the initiative in setting forth the terms of the transaction; we keep the followers moving toward their goal in the transaction when the going gets rough. We dispense rewards commensurate with how our followers have lived up to their part of the bargain.

By contrast, *transforming* leadership (Burns, 1978, p. 20) "occurs when one or more persons *engage* with others in such a way that leaders and followers raise one another to higher levels of motivation and morality." Rather than simply realizing value goals that were known ahead of time, leaders and followers discover within the relationship—be it a social movement or a college course—new values and new human possibilities. I need not dwell on the description of transforming leadership by faculty members, for I suspect that none of us would be here if we had not ourselves had some of those transforming experiences in association with our own teachers.

"Transforming leadership is dynamic leadership in the sense that the leaders throw themselves into a relationship with followers who will feel 'elevated' by it and often become more active themselves, thereby creating new cadres of leaders" (Burns, 1978, p. 20). Of course, those moments of transforming leadership are also those in which the separation of teacher and student is overcome. However, Burns reminds us, leaders remain leaders in light of their ability to address themselves to the needs of followers, needs that are unperceived or poorly articulated by the followers themselves.

Buber's I–Thou Relationships. Tom's three models of the teacher-student relationship, and Burns's distinction between the merely transactional and the truly transforming possibilities of the leader-follower relationship, point to the qualitative essence of the teacher-student relationship at its best. But the person who most helped me see these possibilities is Martin Buber in his book *I and Thou*.

Briefly, Buber (1958, pp. 9–11) distinguishes between "I–it" relationships in which the "it" is a means to an end, and "I–Thou" relationships in which we confront an other, directly and concretely, with our whole being in a stance of mutual disclosure—honestly, without any attempt to manipulate and for the purpose of the relationship: "to body it forth," not to capture the other for analytic understanding. The relationships of lovers and ultimately the human person's relationship to God best exemplify the I–Thou relationship. Buber finds more limited possibilities for I–Thou relationships in the immediacy of a relationship with a pet or with a work of art.

In a postscript to *I and Thou* written forty years after its original appearance, Buber discusses the relationship between teacher and student as a very special case of an I–Thou relationship. It is special because it is asymmetrical. For the teacher, the relationship must be marked by what Buber (1958, p. 132) calls "inclusion" (*Umfassung*), the realization of the student in his or her wholeness. "In order to help the realization of the best potentialities in the pupil's life, the teacher must really *mean* him as the definite person he is in his potentiality, and his actuality; more precisely, he must not know him as a mere sum of qualities, strivings and inhibitions, he must be aware of him as a whole being and affirm him in that wholeness. But he can only do this if he meets him again and again as his partner in a bipolar situation."

No matter how well the student grasps the special quality of the relationship, "the special educative relationship could not persist if the pupil for his part practiced 'inclusion,' that is, if he lived the teacher's part in the common situation" (Buber, 1958, p. 132). For Buber, the educative relationship precludes full mutuality. Of course, a teacher and a student can become friends (or lovers) and realize the full mutuality of that relationship, but then—and this is important—the specific educational relationship is lost.

Thus, the basic ethical task of teaching is twofold. First, it involves making the effort to come to know the student in that person's wholeness, a process that inevitably requires considerable disclosure of our own selves, with all of the anxiety that may involve. Second, the relationship requires a careful "holding back," a certain detachment on the part of the teacher, similar to that of the therapist.

Ethical Obligations that Derive from the Teacher-Student Relationship. It is not easy to find the balance of disclosure and reserve described above. We know that faculty members do not always try to engage students as whole persons. We also know of cases where close relationships are established, but the special asymmetry necessary for an educational relationship is neglected or sacrificed for the sake of the full interpersonal mutuality of love or friendship.

We can begin to imagine other ethical obligations that come from this understanding of the teacher-student relationship as the full engagement of persons. I have already mentioned the need for self-disclosure. We must learn to distinguish precious moments when the student question "But what do you really think?" is asked in the earnestness and engagement of I and Thou from those occasions when the same question is asked in a cheap way as part of an I–it effort to manipulate the teacher, to "psych him out" as my generation would have said. We must be prepared to respond appropriately to these two different modes of relationship.

Another obligation that follows from an understanding of the teacher-student relationship as the meeting of full persons is genuine listening. Listening requires patience, even in the face of the imperatives of "coverage." Listening means that we must sometimes delay gratifying our urges to make an encouraging or critical or witty response to earnest but poorly articulated student comments. Sometimes it is better to keep our awesome brilliance to ourselves.

A third obligation that falls upon us if we are to try to meet the student in his or her complete individuality is that we must celebrate—not merely tolerate—that person's uniqueness. Differences between our own selves and the very selves of students represent challenges to mutual understanding, and the process of mutual self-disclosure *takes time*. This is why establishing the relationship of trust and understanding requires personal meeting "again and again," as Buber stresses.

In 1987, the Society for Values in Higher Education distributed a questionnaire to about thirty of its Fellows (college and university professors from institutions throughout the country) who had experience in mentoring African-American or Hispanic students, either as assigned advisors or informally as concerned teachers. The most important point of consensus within the group of respondents (which included two Hispanic and two African-American colleagues) was that mentoring minority students required more time than mentoring other students. Additional time was required to develop an atmosphere of continually growing trust in order to bring out crucial information about personal and intellectual backgrounds, values, and aspirations. Several experienced mentors asserted that only after some of this mutual process of self-disclosure was well underway and certain differences had been identified—indeed celebrated—did students reveal the deep anxieties and hopes that needed to be addressed in competent advising. Here again, this exploration of an ideal model of the teacher-student relationship and its corollary, the positive appreciation of diversity, suggest a concrete obligation on us as to how we allocate our precious time. Once we accept this obligation, it becomes one more competing claim on our time, and not necessarily one that is rewarded when given priority or is punished when neglected.

Finally, we think of the student-teacher relationship as the meeting of complete persons. We may also find helpful the phrase with which Alan Tom entitles his book: teaching as a moral craft. Tom contends that teaching is a moral activity because of the moral dimension of the student-teacher relationship and because of the moral basis of the curriculum. Teaching is a *moral* activity because the classroom is permeated by a moral order that has consequences for persons (Tom, 1984, p. 95). It is a *craft* because it is learned by a combination of experience and the application of knowledge gained by others to specific situations. It requires the "ability to think synthetically, both internal to craft considerations and between craft and context" (Tom, 1984, pp. 109ff). Tom recognizes some similarities between the activities of the teacher and those of the artist, but opts for the metaphor of teaching as a craft because the metaphor of teaching as an art focuses too heavily on the aesthetic fittingness of what we do.

Day-to-day Ethical Issues

With the concept of teaching as a moral craft in hand, and the ideal of the teacher-student relationship as one between full persons, I turn now to four norms that govern many of the specifics of teachers' actions in the teaching relationship. These norms are honesty, promise-keeping, respect for persons, and fairness. I certainly believe that these norms must govern the conduct of students as well as teachers, but I focus my remarks on teachers' conduct. It is, of course, part of teachers' responsibility as role models to take the lead in demonstrating conduct in accord with these norms.

Honesty requires little elaboration; it is a norm whose importance to the endeavor of teaching and learning is immediately apparent. I do not think that faculty honesty in the classroom is a major issue. When charges of dishonesty are made against faculty members, the issues usually involve use and attribution of research or campus politics, not conduct in the classroom. I think that teachers do much better on this norm than on the others.

Promise-keeping is a norm that is often violated, in my observation. Our syllabi, assignments, and class and office hour schedules involve promises to students. We gripe plenty when the rules are changed on *us* in the middle of the game—the criteria for tenure and promotion, for example. Do we recognize that students might have similar feelings? When we must break some of those implicit promises for legitimate personal or pedagogic reasons, do we acknowledge the seriousness of our action and try to explain the overriding reasons?

Respect for persons, our third norm, comes into play in many day-to-day situations. Practicing common courtesy is a necessary, if low level, consequence of this norm, but I must say that I have occasionally observed or experienced a lack of simple courtesy on the part of teachers toward students. If the teacher-student relationship is (at least potentially) a *special* interpersonal relationship as I contend, how ironic it is if we fail to observe even the ordinary standards of courtesy in our dealings with students by apologizing for missed appointments and responding promptly to students' needs for guidance and feedback.

The concept of respect for persons requires further elaboration and application. In his derivation of this imperative from the Christian ideal of agape, Gene Outka (1972, p. 261) notes that the concept of equal regard for persons means that we owe human persons regard universally and apart from acquired excellences. Further, I have been persuaded by Charles Reynolds (1990) that the norm of respect for persons also entails the responsibility to be compassionate and to strive to enhance the self-worth of other persons. Or, as Joseph Katz (1988, p. 177) put it, "there are far too many students in our courses for whom learning has been a humiliating experience. . . . It is remarkable in how many ways teachers unwittingly exacerbate [students'] lack of self-esteem."

In our struggles against student ignorance and indolence, our justifiable critique of student work (or lack thereof) may be presented in ways that erode self-worth. I do not underestimate the difficulty of balancing the requirements of candor, which flow from the norm of honesty, with the requirements of enhancing self-esteem. This difficulty points to the need for the quality of good judgment in a teacher. There are no simple formulas for resolving all of the moral claims upon us, but to act without alertness to the norms that are at stake is unprofessional for practitioners of a moral craft.

Some of the most hotly debated issues in teaching today involve these collisions of moral claims. I think particularly of the controversies on many campuses about racist and sexist comments by students, in or out of the classroom. Here the value of freedom of expression collides with the value of maintaining a community of mutual respect that makes learning possible. Forbidding students to express their ignorant prejudices will not necessarily eliminate those prejudices, but ignoring expressions of prejudice when they occur in your classroom—as they have in mine—is impermissible according to the norm of respect for persons.

Here again I have no neat resolution to all of the issues. I do believe that unless we use our moral imagination to fully envision what is involved in respect for persons and then have the courage and good judgment to make this norm vivid to our students, a rather cheap version of the value of freedom of speech will carry the day—to the real detriment of our communities of learning and our wider society.

Fairness is the fourth and final norm for our moral craft. Normally we pride ourselves in our ability to be fair, and we recognize that the challenge of living up to the norm of fairness is that of overcoming our subjective preferences and our likes and dislikes. We know that fairness demands a certain objectivity in how we deal with students, and particularly in how we assess their achievements. We are also aware of the power of our personal preferences and acknowledge that we have strong capacities to delude ourselves into thinking that we have eliminated subjectivity from our professional judgments. I trust that we read examinations without first looking at the name of the author and fight the temptations of graphological identification that a stack of bluebooks may prompt.

In my early days as a teacher, I used to evaluate my students' contribution to class discussion at the end of the semester—the famous fudge factor. Since then, I have decided that I should not rely on my informal recollections of their achievements over many weeks in assigning this grade, but should (in the case of a seminar or discussion class) review after every class what each student may have contributed, keeping notes about the nature and quality of their comments and questions. Writing up and ordering these notes takes a bit of time, and when I assign the term discussion grade after reviewing them at the end of term, the mark is rarely far from what I would have given lacking that documentation. Yet I regard the time and effort as well spent, a safeguard to my own capability for selective memory or the concoction of pure subjective fudge.

Broader Ethical Obligations

In their *The Ethical Investor,* Simon, Powers, and Gunneman (1972) reviewed the Kew Gardens murder case and offered an analysis that has since become a classic. You may recall the circumstances. For almost an hour Kitty Genovese was pursued by an assailant in an apartment complex. She was stabbed repeatedly and her screams were heard by many people, yet no one called the police; no one wanted to get involved. In their analysis of the incident, the authors distinguish four kinds of responsibility that applied to the situation. In this case, the actions that might have flowed from each did not occur, and the result was Ms. Genovese's death. In a less dramatic way, the same four types of responsibility may fall upon us in our relations with students.

The first type of responsibility is *causal responsibility*: if we cause a harm, we are obliged to try to correct it.

The second type of responsibility is *role responsibility*. In the Kew Gardens case, the police had the professional role of providing security to a citizen but were not on hand when they were needed. In the case of moral responsibility toward students, almost everything I have said so far about our obligations has been said in the context of role responsibility.

The third type of responsibility is the *responsibility of proximity*. At Kew Gardens, physical proximity created an awareness of Ms. Genovese's need and thus an imperative to help, *even for those who did not cause the harm or have role responsibility for her safety.* Similarly, with an extended sense of proximity, we may as individuals become aware of urgent needs of our students and have responsibility to address them, even when taking this responsibility is not "part of our job." A student may come to a teacher with a serious problem, undefined as to whether it is an academic problem, a problem of mental health, or a spiritual problem. We have the obligation to address the problem and not to narrow the diagnosis to its academic aspects just because that may suit us. The best course of action may well be the equivalent of calling the police—that is, referring the problem to someone whose professional training provides the role responsibility for helping the student.

Finally, there is the *responsibility of last resort.* When all else fails, it may fall to us to render help if tragedy is to be avoided. Situations of this sort are rare, fortunately, but I mention the responsibility of last resort in this effort to complete my map of our moral responsibilities.

Teaching and learning are thus processes of moving together toward human wholeness. Ethics are not an add-on to a values-neutral craft. They are implicit in every aspect of our teaching and learning practices, as presented in more detail by the authors of the following chapters covering interpersonal relationships, classroom conduct, and administrative relationships.

The very nature of our practice, then, demands that we reflect upon it as an ethical project. Several chapters of this volume offer principles, decision models, and guidelines for the reflective educator. These tools remind us of the essence of our craft and help us sort through the practical challenges we face.

Moreover, these challenges pertain to the larger educational enterprise in which not only individual souls but also, as Socrates well understood, the character of our public life are at stake. In reenergizing our commitment to the demands of our craft, reflection on the ethical dimension of teaching becomes a source of self renewal and, ideally, public renewal as well. Like Socrates, we should hope to arise in the morning with the sense of the import of our choices.

References

Bloom, A. *The Closing of the American Mind: How Higher Education Has Failed Democracy and Impoverished the Souls of Today's Students.* New York: Simon and Schuster, 1987.

Buber, M. *I and Thou.* New York: Charles Scribner's Sons, 1958.

Burns, J. M. *Leadership.* New York: Harper & Row, 1978.

Freire, P. *Pedagogy of the Oppressed.* New York: Seabury, 1970.

Katz, J. "Does Teaching Help Students Learn?" In B. A. Kimball (ed.), *Teaching Undergraduates.* Buffalo, N.Y.: Prometheus Books, 1988.

Outka, G. *Agape: an Ethical Analysis.* New Haven, Conn.: Yale University Press, 1972.

Plato, *Protagoras.* Translated by W. K. C. Guthrie. Harmondsworth, U.K.: Penguin, 1956.

Reynolds, C., and Smith, D. "Academic Principles of Responsibility." In W. W. May (ed.), *Ethics and Higher Education.* New York: American Council on Education, 1990.

Simon, J. G., Powers, C. W., and Gunneman, J. P. *The Ethical Investor.* New Haven, Conn.: Yale University Press, 1972.

Tom, A. *Teaching as a Moral Craft.* New York: Longman, 1984.

DAVID C. SMITH *is president of the Council for Ethics in Economics (Columbus, Ohio) and former executive director of the Society for Values in Higher Education.*

Students' developmental stages affect their capacities to comprehend and absorb difficult texts and the moral problems embedded in them, and we should teach accordingly. Such attention to subjects whose identities are in flux will inevitably turn into transformations for both student and teacher.

Teaching the *Subject*: Developmental Identities in Teaching

Mary Burgan

Surely one of the ethical responsibilities of teachers is to know their subject, but *subject* can have a multiplicity of meanings in the pedagogical context. The subject can be the field of knowledge, or—from the point of view of psychology—*subject* may refer to the student as a psychic entity. Especially in object-relations psychology, a post-Freudian elaboration of childhood development, the subject is theorized as a formation derived from the relations between the infant and the mother's body, the techniques of basic early care, and the dynamics of specific families in particular cultures. Under such a view, the individual is *subjected* to shifting versions of a self. Young persons, for example, are constructed within a web of conflicting demands and rejections as they try to resolve some provisional identity for themselves. This notion of the self is one source of the "postmodern awareness of the fragmentary and fluid nature of human identity" that David C. Smith (see Chapter One) has mentioned as a condition of our teaching. Our reflections on the moral dimensions of teaching often center on stable philosophical verities and unchanging human nature. We will do well to think also of what developmental psychology should add to an ethical consideration of what we do.

In this chapter I will discuss the ways in which college teachers may enter into subjective *transactions* with their students. I assume that such transactions, when they reach an interpersonal or mentoring phase, will inevitably turn into *transformations* for both student and teacher. If students are subjects whose identities are in flux, so are their teachers. Thus, even the professor's *refusal* to be moved by his or her students' needs can become a part of the interaction of mutually developing subjectivities for good or for ill.

I will emphasize three aspects of these intersubjective elements of teaching here. First, I will sketch the developmental theories that form my assumptions.

In laying out this theoretical base, I make no claims to expertise in psychology. Rather, I speak from my general interest in the work of developmentalists encountered in my research and teaching. I have used Erik Erikson's (1950, 1968) developmental scheme as a key to the interpretation of adolescent literature (Burgan, 1988). I have also found useful the elaborations of his work on *stages* by other psychologists such as William Perry (1970), Lawrence Kohlberg (Power, Higgins, and Kohlberg, 1989), and Carol Gilligan (1982), even though I am uneasy with the neatness of some of their formulations.

After outlining my understanding of such psychological insight, I suggest some learning situations in which students' developmental stages may make a radical difference in their capacities to comprehend and absorb difficult texts and the moral problems embedded in them. Finally, I discuss my own sense of the ways in which teaching should transform the subjectivities of teachers themselves.

Students and Stages

I center my discussion on the traditional, late-adolescent student, even though it is now true that the age norms in college classes, especially classes in urban settings, comprehensive universities, and community colleges, have become unpredictable. There are many students who return to our classes after years of absence, and many students who now begin college as "freshmen" may be in their late twenties.

In Erikson's writing, attention to the developmental issue of identity is reserved for adolescence, but it can be valid through many variations in age and experience. All novices share the feelings of adolescents as they begin a new world of learning. Furthermore, throughout adulthood most individuals can be seen to be involved in some developmental stage that builds upon early identity formation. They may be preoccupied with the tasks of discovering what kind of parent they want to be by testing their identities against those of their own parents. They may be critically involved in making sense of their achievements at the end of their productive years as mothers or workers. Or they may have foreclosed the process of self-definition so adamantly in earlier years of social or economic struggle that their current educational striving has become an angry defense against identity disturbance. Understanding the threat that education may bring to identity can help us to react wisely rather than to form our own defensive classifications of our students. Thus, the mandate to pay attention to developmental stages holds, whatever the ages of those we teach.

In Erik Erikson's (1950, 1968) eight-stage scheme of psychosocial development, adolescence is squarely at the center. Erikson posits the three Freudian foundational stages (oral, anal, and genital) as based upon more or less passive bodily capabilities that progressively permit the child to differentiate from the parental figure and to assert independence. But Erikson's contribution is to move beyond the Freudian triad to delineate the stages a child must engage during the school age and after.

The originality of Erikson's thinking becomes clear as he emphasizes the playing out of roles as the work of childhood—noting that identity is built upon a sense of competence, of being up to the tasks of life, of being able to master them. Erikson sees the individual as an active participant in this learning, responding with an essentially healthy instinct to master the rules of the various childhood games that are replicated in the intellectual experience of schooling and in the social testing of making a place for oneself with peers.

In adolescence, the learning of school continues, but added to it are the more complicated issues of how to be an individual in a confusing social world. Erikson sees an essentially productive confusion arising from the young person's need to formulate a life plan without being forced prematurely into confining social roles. One of the primary instruments of testing in this stage involves the formation of loyalties to groups that are in rebellion against adult expectations. Adolescence is a time of conversion—to religion, to fads in music and dress, and to groups that demand some surrender of the self in return for security. Erikson is convincing in his counsel of patience with such transitory behaviors, for he understands the exercise of identity crisis as positive, so long as it does not lead individuals into the kinds of role-playing that may lock them into a diagnosis of neurosis or abnormality from which there is no escape. Erikson urges mentoring adults—teachers, psychologists, judges—to avoid defining young people by name-calling. So eager are adolescents for definition that being called "stupid" or "cute" or "brilliant" or "bad" by an adult may place them in a lifelong effort to live up to the name tag.

From the fulcrum of adolescence, a period that has been prolonged in sophisticated cultures that require extended apprenticeships, Erikson moves to the last three stages that ensue through adulthood. In the earliest of these, blending with late adolescence, the individual becomes capable of intimacy with one other person—leaving the security of group loyalties to venture into the risks of single partnerships. From such partnerships follows the next stage, in which the individual is safe enough in psychosocial identity to begin to care about the future. Erikson finds caretaking ("generativity") to be the defining virtue of maturity, and he expands this idea beyond the obvious biological exercise of childbearing to include teaching and other creative work. Finally, Erikson suggests that old age constitutes a stage in itself, one with its own crises and tasks. The biological crisis is death, which poses the psychological challenge to build upon the successful transition from the earlier stages in order to surrender the grandiose claims of the self to immortality. The characteristic pathology of old age is the temptation to despair, and Erikson reads that temptation as deriving from the tragedy of failure to secure identity throughout the earlier stages of development.

Mastery is the key in Erikson's sense of the way young people develop. Although he emphasizes the determining social factors in the way such mastery is encouraged or repressed (as in the ways various Native American cultures handle the swaddling of infants), he also seeks some margin for the variations caused by genetic endowment, particular family styles, and singular psychic events. Thus, the identity stage is a critical one in which a plethora of influences bear down upon the developing person. There are the demands of the clan, the equally pressing pull of peers, the intellectual imperative to find an appropriate and satisfying creed to live by, and the increasing impulses to sexual activity—all of which play out in bodies that have changed and are changing in ways that can be both gratifying and disturbing.

Implications for College Teaching

For those of us who teach students who have just graduated from high school, the revelation that late adolescents tend to be, still, merely "subjects" comes as no surprise. Every day, we see that many of them are not yet possessed of self-knowledge, of habits of premeditation, or (according to some contemporary developmental theories) of the cognitive flexibility and range to grasp complexity in judging moral situations. When teaching is considered the transmission of simple, basic facts and principles, the teacher may not need profound insight into the student's subjectivity. But teaching is seldom so simple, and college teachers, whose students are frequently at this critical stage in maturation, seem ethically bound to understand their students' developmental capacities, and to teach accordingly.

Erikson's thinking on adolescence was extremely influential in the late sixties and early seventies because it addressed massive cultural changes that preoccupied a nation whose divisions were mirrored in generational conflict. We might surmise that such conflict has by now gone underground. Our campuses are quiet, our students are more worried about getting jobs than manning the barricades, and the new seriousness of many of these worried souls carries with it a kind of conservatism that disdains the haphazard experimentation of the generations just before their own. That some identity experimentation still holds can be surmised not only on the basis of psychological theory but also by current fads. It explains the delight that post-adolescents now take in the *Far Side* cartoons of Gary Larson and the undermining of traditional stereotypes by *The Simpsons*. The flamboyant dislocations of grunge and the rancor of rap embody the anger and depression of brand name yuppiedom where there are no idealistic roles to play. The nostalgic community surrounding the Grateful Dead betokens a longing for tradition without the rigidity of rules—this longing made manifest by an outpouring of sadness that crossed several generations at the death of Jerry Garcia.

I believe that such cultural happenings indicate that the adolescents who inhabit our introductory classrooms are frequently divided in subjectivity. They need the security of a promising cultural identity, even as they confront an imperative to open themselves to varieties of experimentation while seeking a place uniquely their own. Current theoretical trends that emphasize the social constructedness of identities may find it easier to encourage adolescents' experimentation than to foster adherence to the formative loyalties to their families, local customs, and religious traditions. Indeed, students' reaction to such encouragement by increased entrenchment in creeds may signify the pressure they feel. The ethical question for teachers in areas in which issues of subjectivity are paramount, such as literature, psychology and philosophy, is how to accommodate the embedded relativism of contemporary thought without encouraging the drifting student never to settle, never to resolve, never to take a stand.

How do we meet the needs of such students without becoming amateur therapists or self-help gurus? I believe that we do it through maintaining our own roles as knowledgeable mentors who can coach them into mastery. From my talks with students (among whom I number my own children during their recent college years), I find that their estimates of good teaching coincide with developmental needs. They rightfully expect their professors to fulfill two basic expectations. One is competence in knowing. The other is caring about whether or not their "subjects" learn.

I have suggested a distinction between instruction and teaching, but now I want to withdraw that distinction because I believe that any kind of transfer of knowledge or expertise will have an impact on the psychic development of students. If the transfer of information is successful, it provides the adolescent student with an immense boost in self-confidence that is extremely powerful when the information leads to a level of skill that can be tested, relied upon, and put to use. Thus, teachers who are dry and distant but who insist on mastery can be extremely influential. They meet the recurrent need of adolescents to strengthen their identities by increasing their capacities to understand difficult concepts and practice difficult tasks. On the other hand, teachers who eliminate challenging texts or tasks may underestimate the urges of their students to take on learning.

The urge to mastery that Erikson suggests as a feature of early schooling remains a significant feature of an adolescent identity crisis. We can see this in the urgency with which the young men in the film *Hoop Dreams* practice basketball. We can see it in the fervor of young women who spend hours learning the step dances of their sororities. And there are scores of young musicians who heed Thoreau's boast of marching to a different drummer by becoming drummers themselves. Their hours of practice in the basements and garages of their long-suffering parents illustrate the adolescent need to establish a special identity through mastery. And consider the computer nerds who spend hours unravelling software and playing esoteric games. Their entry into virtual reality is frequently an effort to establish their own reality through a smart ingenuity.

No one should underestimate the toil that such expertise costs or the identity gains that it provides. Thus, the computer science teacher, the engineer, and the dance instructor can provide essential identity reinforcement to students when they help them gain access to skill. My point here is that knowledge is power, and teachers who worry about the ethics of their relations to students sometimes forget that fact. They forget that the most important feature of their address to their classes may be what they have to teach, rather than their ability to spellbind or to amuse. Adolescents who are challenged to learn and who are taught in such a way that they can learn are provided with an essential developmental power. Their teacher's knowledge is a critically reassuring factor in such learning experiences.

I suggest that the most ethical thing a teacher can do, in light of the beginning student's developmental needs, is to know the field and to find ways to present it as clearly as possible. The teacher's job is to present doable challenges. Nothing is so lethal to a young person's sense of capacity to learn as to be confronted with an incomprehensible subject in a chaotic way.

It is also true that teaching is not simply "learning methodology" and teachers are not mere podium images. They cannot be replaced by television, for example, or by computer screens. One reason that a live teacher must be in charge of learning is that adolescent students need confirmation by an adult mentor. Thus, the second critical feature that students tend to note in successful teachers is that they care about their students. I do not believe that caring has to be a personal invasion of the student's life, but it must be a commitment to recognize the young or the ignorant as deserving of instruction and attention.

Recently I met a graduate of my university who wanted to reminisce with me about his undergraduate days. He told me about his English professor and how demanding she had been in the two classes he took from her. He was not resentful; indeed, he admired her because she was the only teacher he could not fool. He told the story of one day in the last week before his graduation when he had passed her on the street and she had looked up, recognized him from two years before, and said "Hi." "She knew who I was," he told me. "I just couldn't believe that she would know who I was!"

Of course, there are ways to go further by design, and settings where more personal contact is warranted. In these settings I believe that the teacher can be a more effective mentor by recognizing the identity issues that students face. I will give one example from my own teaching.

A number of years ago, I was teaching a women's studies course, and I had just read Carol Gilligan's *In a Different Voice* (1982), a study that looks at the gender dimensions of adolescent development. This book helped me to see that undergraduate women in my classes rarely spoke up, that they had lost their voices in some way. On the first meeting of a special honor section of my lecture class, I asked each member to introduce herself. As I went around the circle of young women—all valedictorians of their high school classes—I realized that I could not hear their names. My first reaction was to wonder if I were losing my hearing (a reflex action for someone at my stage in the developmental cycle!). I soon realized, however, that these students had so little confidence that they could not identify themselves openly in public. I told the young women that I wanted to go around one more time, but this time I wanted each student to tell her name in a voice loud enough for everyone to hear.

It was a casual exercise, I thought, but it brought two profoundly moving results. One student changed her name later in the semester. She had come to college as a young mother, married to the father of her child because of the expectations of both of their families, and was working very hard to get through school with a new baby. She told the class that she realized that guilt for getting pregnant had caused her to take her husband's surname and to reject her high school name "Cassie" as too frivolous for the delinquent identity that she must live down. She had decided to go back to Cassie and her maiden name because she had become more sure of who she was, more accepting of her total identity.

The second result of the discussions of names and identities in that course occurred just this year when an e-mail message from one of the students appeared on my screen out of the blue. She was writing from another town in another state. She said, "Hi. I still remember your class. And I want you to know that whenever anyone asks me who I am now, I say my name out loud and clear."

The Teacher's Role

The developmental paradigm is multifaceted. As I confirmed the right of my women students to speak their names, so one of those students confirmed for me the power of my vocation as a teacher. But the two-way nature of the interaction can cause problems if we as teachers fail to think of ourselves as "subjects" in a complex interaction of generational identities.

I can illustrate the problems this interaction may pose by recounting my critique of a freshman English class taught by two graduate students several years ago. These teaching assistants described their course in a panel on pedagogy at an annual symposium for faculty and graduate students in my department. They were presenting their answer to the question of bringing literary theory of the deconstructionist kind into the freshman classroom. The text for their class was a chapter on amnesia from Oliver Sacks's book *The Man Who Mistook His Wife for a Hat* (1985). In this chapter, Sacks describes the plight of an amnesiac whose lack of memory causes him to engage in endless storytelling about himself—reconstructing new identities in an endless flow of language in which there is never any connection with the actualities of his life. Sacks diagnoses this incessant linguistic creation of alternate identities as lacking in affect, oblivious to the boredom of listeners, and incapable of structuring any conclusions. The young teachers interpreted the condition of this patient as a remarkable illustration of the current theories that tell the truth about modern experience as fractional and irrational. Their goal in teaching Sacks to adolescents was to enforce the similarity of ordinary experience to the situation of amnesia and thus to shake their students out of their commonsense notions of history, psychic stability, and the referentiality of language.

In my critique, I responded vigorously with my own reading of Sacks. I insisted that he was telling the story of a profoundly ill patient whose inability to connect with the social reality of his present and the autobiographical reality of his past was by no means a sponsored model of the postmodern condition. Further, I questioned the appropriateness of such efforts to disabuse adolescent students of their slavish trust in common perception. How, I asked these young teachers, do you *know* that your students are so complacent in their apprehension of stable identities? No matter how calmly they sit before you, I suggested, many of them are facing significant questions about their hold on reality. From my own teaching of *The Bell Jar,* Sylvia Plath's memoir of a suicidal late adolescence (1971), I had discovered that over half of my students who were in the twenty-something age range had contemplated suicide in their teens. Using this finding, I came very close to accusing the two apprentice teachers of gross irresponsibility in assuming that they knew their subjects. I insisted that my interpretation of Sacks would be more relevant to the needs of the freshman mind because it emphasized the *integrative* power of memory. And I pointed to another story in the collection in which a Korsakov's Syndrome patient had some relief in partial memory, and further solace in music and the quiet of daily Mass. Why would their teaching fasten on pathology as the norm, neglecting the celebration of the human impulse to equilibrium in Sacks's wonderful book?

I hope that this account gives some flavor of my mood as I sought to refute the concept of identity these novice teachers wanted to present. I realize now, however, that my own role as a wise defender of the needs of adolescents blinded me, in turn, to the needs of their young teachers. After all, the teaching assistants I attacked were in their late twenties—less than a generation older than most of the students in their classes! It is no wonder that they took what I said as a frontal attack on what they had learned and embraced as a liberating doctrine that could unveil the coercive power of forced roles. They prosecuted such a view with passion because, perhaps, they were enacting their own experiments with identity.

I also neglected the impact of my own power as a senior professor (and at that time I was chair of my department) intent on putting the young in their place. Feeling isolated by my resistance to this new theorizing, I insisted on holding forth—displaying my mastery of Sacks's book and of current theoretical tendencies. I now realize that I was threatened by the self-assurance of these young teachers—not so much in their failure to calculate the psychological needs of their students as in their advocacy of a theoretical view that I found threatening because it might displace everything I had learned and believed. In pouncing upon their ideology, I was forgetting how needful to them—entrants to a field of intense theoretical struggle—would be the mastery of a system, its absorption into experience, and their inevitable adjustment of it to their own needs. I was attacking not only their reading of Oliver Sacks but their identity as scholars. Until these two bright and effective young teachers left our graduate program, I found myself avoiding them in the hallways, feeling guilty about what I had done.

The problem was, of course, that in trying to understand the developmental stage of freshman students, I forgot my own developmental stage. I believe that I was right to call these teaching assistants to account for their misreading of their students and of Sacks, but my critique was so flavored by indignation that it cut off further communication. I regret that effect, but I also realize that my resistance may have been a necessary move in this complicated minuet of generations. A failure to respond critically would have been a forfeiture of my own role, for as the senior teacher in the constellation, it was incumbent upon me to take what they said seriously enough to respond. It is more important to speak than to keep a resentful, elderly silence, fearing to be named a theoretical has-been by trendy students and colleagues. In such quarrels between the young and the old, it may be more productive to maintain enough openness to keep the exchange in play than to determine who is right and who is wrong.

If the identities of college students are in flux, is it the teacher's role to encourage a spectrum of possibilities, carefully maintaining neutrality as to which might be more desirable? Or should teachers become a "still point in the turning world" upon which students' experiments in selfhood can be tried? Or does the role of the teacher change according to his or her own stage? Are the urges for identity in the flux and flow of role experimentation among adolescents so strong that whether we choose so or not, we ourselves become part of an identity crisis when we enter into the classroom and—more significantly—when we undertake a mentoring relationship with particular students? With all of the development that it is our pleasure to observe in our students, young or old, we may be oblivious to the changes that can take place in ourselves. Our ethical imperative is to cultivate the wisdom to recognize who we are and where we are in the cycle—and to act our age.

References

Burgan, M. "The Question of Work: Adolescent Literature and the Eriksonian Paradigm." *Children's Literature in Education,* 1988, 19.4, 187–98.

Erikson, E. H. *Childhood and Society.* New York: Norton, 1950.

Erikson, E. H. *Identity, Youth, and Crisis.* New York: Norton, 1968.

Gilligan, C. *In a Different Voice: Psychological Theory and Women's Development.* Cambridge, Mass.: Harvard University Press, 1982.

Perry, W. G. *Forms of Intellectual and Ethical Development in the College Years.* New York: Holt, Rinehart & Winston, 1970.

Plath, S. *The Bell Jar.* New York: Harper, 1971.

Power, F. C., Higgins, A., and Kohlberg, L. *Lawrence Kohlberg's Approach to Moral Education.* New York: Columbia University Press, 1989.

Sacks, O. *The Man Who Mistook His Wife for a Hat and Other Clinical Tales.* New York: Summit, 1985.

MARY BURGAN is general secretary of the American Association of University Professors (Washington, D.C.). She formerly was professor and chair of English and associate dean of arts and sciences at Indiana University.

Although the primary setting for the student-teacher relationship is the classroom, an important ethical task is to handle the relationship well outside of the classroom. May Sarton's novel The Small Room *depicts both success and failure in this task.*

The Ethics of Student-Faculty Friendships

Richard L. Baker, Jr.

> The relation between student and teacher must be about the most complex and ill-defined there is.
>
> —May Sarton, *The Small Room*

Many authors, as well as many campus ethics committees, try to ascertain the ethics of the student-teacher relationship without first seeking an adequate definition of it. Take, for example, Steven M. Cahn's widely-read book, *Saints and Scamps: Ethics in Academia* (1986). Cahn holds that the teacher should prepare thoroughly, make clear in-class presentations, devise suitably specific assignments, and grade promptly and fairly. At the same time, he prohibits student-faculty friendships, insisting that faculty must remain "dispassionate," avoiding "even the appearance of partiality" (1986, p. 35). As Cahn sees it, a teacher should "not seek to be their [the students'] psychiatrist, friend, or lover" (1986, p. 36). Similarly, Peter Markie warns that "we must not be friends with our students" because such friendships "conflict with our fundamental obligations as professors" (1994, p. 70). Foremost among such obligations seem to be competent instruction, unbiased grading, and "running the competition" for "class rank, honors, and job opportunities" (1994, p. 74). Indeed, to protect such obligations Markie warns us to avoid even "casual" social relationships with students beyond class.

All of this may seem unexceptionable at first glance, but consider the implicit conception of the student-teacher relationship that underlies Cahn's

The epigraph and other quotations throughout the chapter are from *The Small Room* by May Sarton. Copyright 1961 by May Sarton. Reprinted by permission of W. W. Norton & Company, Inc.

and Markie's injunctions. The teacher is expected to present class material well, grade fairly, and abjure any other form of relationship with students. Combine these, and the student-teacher relationship becomes one in which the teacher is nothing more than an information dispenser and grader, and the student nothing more than a receiver and gradee. The professor becomes a kind of living encyclopedia or sorting mechanism for the meritocracy.

I would like to propose a more explicit and, I think, more adequate conception of the relationship. Cahn and many others lay down a set of rules to insure minimal moral competence. In contrast, my approach will be to hold up models of ethical excellence. As Martha Nussbaum (1992) writes in the *Encyclopedia of Ethics,* an increasing number of moral philosophers in the past thirty-five years have turned to literature to discover models of excellence and to develop the meanings of ethical terms. In this spirit, I will use a novel—May Sarton's *The Small Room* (1961)—to define the student-teacher relationship and to consider the ethics pertaining to it.

I choose Sarton's novel because it provides, as one critic puts it, "an intensely interesting analysis of the college teacher's job" (Sibley, 1972, p. 127). The essence of that job, according to Sarton's heroine, is "the care of [the students'] souls" (p. 165). Out of context, this phrase may seem platitudinous, so it is important to consider it in terms of the action and characters of the novel. By so doing, I hope to show that the student-teacher relationship is a unique kind of friendship. It is a friendship in that the professor acts for the good of the student without ulterior motive. It is unique in that its passion and intimacy are best expressed through the medium of a subject. The primary setting for this friendship is the classroom, but it should not be restricted exclusively to that venue. Indeed, an important ethical challenge is how to handle this relationship outside the classroom. Cahn and others are rightly concerned about inappropriate intimacy—especially romantic relationships—outside the classroom. I will show, however, that the relationship can be damaged as much by inappropriate distance as by inappropriate intimacy.

I realize that speaking of friendship between professors and students carries some negative connotations, most notably favoritism and inappropriate fraternization. Nonetheless I would like to retain the term and expand its range of meaning. I retain the term because I cannot find a better one to capture the kind of concern, as well as the unique kind of passion and intimacy, that should characterize the relationship. I will begin to expand its meaning by tracing the term back to its classical predecessor (*philia*) and by considering Aristotle's concept of friendship between unequals.

Friendship Between Unequals

In the *Nicomachean Ethics,* Aristotle argues that friendship presupposes equality—equality of age, social position, interests, and, in the case of true friendship, equality of moral virtue. Moreover, in a true friendship there is another kind of equality—a *symmetrical reciprocity*—insofar as each person wants and gives the same things. Each friend wants what is good for the other simply for the

STUDENT-FACULTY FRIENDSHIPS   27

other person's own sake; each friend gives affection to the other. (Indeed, Aristotle considers these to be the distinguishing marks of true friendship.) Aristotle allows, however, that there can be a kind of friendship between *unequals*. It is here that he puts the friendships between parent and child, old and young, ruler and subject, and—alas!—husband and wife. Here, there is an asymmetrical reciprocity. The superior partner gives wisdom, guidance, money, and in general a kind of avuncular concern, whereas the inferior partner gives a kind of affection that incorporates respect and even reverence.

That the professor and student are not equals should be clear enough. The professor is usually older, presumably possesses some knowledge or skill the student lacks, and if nothing else wields the power of the grade book. That the relationship between them is best construed as a *friendship* between unequals, however, requires some explaining. For this, I now turn to *The Small Room*.

The Small Room

The Small Room (1961) is set on the campus of Appleton College in about 1960. Appleton is a small, prestigious women's college that avowedly "prizes excellence" and most emphatically does not offer courses in home economics. Onto this campus comes young Lucy Winter, having recently received her Ph.D. in American Literature from Harvard. She arrives uncertain whether teaching is her true vocation, but certain that she will not have any sort of personal relationships with her students. As she tells an older colleague soon after her arrival, she simply doesn't "believe in personal relationships between teachers and students" (p. 39). The older colleague smiles knowingly, confident that Lucy has a few surprises in store for her.

Friendship in the Classroom. The first surprise is that the student-teacher relationship is a uniquely intimate one. On the first day of class, Lucy decides to throw away her carefully prepared notes and introduce herself by telling the students of her own love for literature and the teachers who inspired that love. As she does so, she discovers that "she could talk to these girls with perfect directness, in a way she had never been able to talk to anyone before in her life." In this "strangely intimate yet impersonal circumstance" Lucy "could give it [the class] something of herself that she would never be able to give to an individual human being" (p. 34).

What Lucy gives of herself here is her passion for literature and the way that literature has shaped her as a person. As a senior colleague tells Lucy, great teachers teach "because a fire burns in their heads" (p. 247). They have a passion for their subject. The truths they encounter there, the beauty they experience, the skills and discipline they develop—all of these bring joy to their lives. The study of their subject has shaped, and continues to shape, their lives. Thus, teaching becomes a kind of self-giving. It involves bringing oneself to the classroom and giving something—often a good deal—of that self away. That same colleague tells Lucy that teaching "takes the marrow out of your bones" (p. 76).

It is here that the teacher meets Aristotle's first criterion of true friendship: the true teacher does not teach for the aggrandizement of her ego or (less likely) for the enrichment of her pocketbook but for the *good* of the other, without ulterior motive and simply for the other person's own sake. The teacher tries to give some of her passion and joy to the students. The teacher's goal is not so much to create a future specialist in the field, but to say, "this has changed my life for the better; perhaps it can do the same for yours."

It is here also that the teacher-student relationship meets Aristotle's criterion for unequal friendship: no matter how good the class, the students simply cannot fully reciprocate such passionate self-giving. For example, after reading the first batch of freshman essays later in the semester, Lucy devotes a class to reading first from the *Iliad* and then from the essays. She compares the majesty of the former with the insipidity of the latter. "This was the material before you and this is how you honored it. . . . Here is one of the great mysterious works of man, as great and mysterious as a cathedral. And what did you do? You gave it so little of your real selves that you actually achieved boredom" (p. 108).

Here Lucy calls on the students to reciprocate—to give more of themselves—and so she should; the essays weren't very good. But the truth is that Lucy will always have more to give. She knows the *Iliad,* and the students do not. It has worked its way into the marrow of her bones, but it has not yet done so (as the essays make depressingly clear) for the students.

So the student-teacher relationship has its own unique *intimacy* (I give something essential of myself) and *passion* (I do so because I care deeply about both the subject and the students). And yet strangely enough, as Lucy herself comes to understand, such passion and intimacy occur in an "impersonal circumstance" through the medium of an "impersonal subject" (pp. 34, 50).

The Wall of the Subject Matter. Late in the fall semester, Lucy is invited to a tea at a student dormitory. She does not relish the prospect, but in the interests of better faculty-student relations, she accepts. Upon her arrival, her worst fears seem confirmed. The setting is stiff and awkward; the students simply gawk at her, unable to engage in even the rudiments of polite conversation.

In desperation, Lucy risks candor. Why did they invite her here? What do they want? So prompted, the students begin to talk more freely. As the discussion proceeds and as the atmosphere more and more becomes that of the classroom, it becomes clear that the students want to get to know the real Lucy Winter as a person. Lucy (somewhat professorially) summarizes their points, saying "what you want is to make contact with the human being, with me myself, not Professor Winter." Although Lucy allows that such contact is "possible sometimes," she suggests that it is difficult as long as the teacher-student relationship is in place. As long as they are professor and students, they need a "third entity" between them. "In the classroom, you see, there are three entities present, you the class, me, and a third far greater than we who fuses us together into a whole. When that third is absent, our real relationship falls apart" (pp. 216–217).

The essential third entity here is the subject matter—the text, if you will. Passion and intimacy can be achieved through this medium, and yet the subject matter also stands in the way of teacher and students having more direct contact with each other. This theme of *mediated intimacy* has been wending its way through the entire novel. Early in the book, at a faculty party, the conversation turns to religion and, in particular, to Simone Weil's comparing the relationship between God and humanity to that of two prisoners in adjacent cells: the wall between them both separates them and enables them to communicate by tapping. A faculty member, returning to the party with volume in hand, reads from Weil directly: "Every separation is a bond" (p. 62). This last phrase stays with Lucy, and by the end of the novel it is clear that she sees the subject matter in the classroom as just this kind of wall, separating her from the students and yet bonding them together, allowing them to be intensely personal through an impersonal medium. And yet occasionally, as Lucy herself discovers during the course of her first semester, the wall will come down.

Friendship Outside the Classroom. The action of the novel revolves around two students, Jane Seaman and Pippa Brentwood. With both, Lucy finds herself—much to her surprise and somewhat reluctantly—in a personal relationship beyond the bounds of the classroom and the scope of her subject.

Jane Seaman, who is enrolled in Lucy's American Renaissance class, is a star student and the protegee of Carryl Cope, by far the most published and most widely renowned member of the faculty. It is Lucy's misfortune to discover that an essay on the *Iliad* that Jane has submitted to the College literary magazine has been plagiarized from a piece by Simone Weil. Lucy immediately recognizes her role as similar to that of a messenger in a Greek tragedy. She has news that no one wants to hear, news that will set in motion a painful and seemingly inexorable chain of events, but news that nonetheless must be told, whatever opprobrium it may bring down on her own head. Yet before she plays out her role, Lucy decides to call Jane into her office to discuss the matter. It would be (as she herself tells Jane) "failing in kindness and in responsibility towards a human being" not to do so (p. 98).

During a difficult, hour-long session, Jane emerges as a joyless, driven, and angry young woman. She speaks of the intense pressure she feels from Carryl Cope to "produce, produce, produce." "The more you do," she says in a level, hateful tone, "the more you're expected to do, and each thing has got to be better, always better" (p. 100). After the conversation, it is clear to Lucy that someone, somewhere has "failed with Jane" (p. 104). Yet Lucy, with a new appreciation for the difficulties of teaching, is hesitant to blame Carryl Cope. During the course of her first semester, Lucy has come to understand that teachers confront half-formed persons, each with a different past and each struggling to grow in her own way. She has come to realize that teachers can have a profound effect on that growth, both for good and bad, often without knowing it. How then can she blame Carryl when she is not at all sure that she is doing—or could do—better? All she can do, as she walks across campus, badly shaken by her conversation with Jane, is feel "the perils of such responsibility" (p. 104).

As perilous as such responsibility may be, Lucy nonetheless takes on even more regarding Jane. When a distraught and slightly drunk Jane shows up on her doorstep later in the semester, Lucy invites her home to New York (Jane has no real home to go to) for the Thanksgiving holiday and persuades her to see a psychiatrist while she is there. Lucy herself recognizes that this is a lot for a first-year teacher to take on. Yet as she sends a sobered and comforted Jane back to the dormitory, Lucy wonders whether "just this were not what you did take on if you chose to be a teacher. . .the care of soul" (p. 165).

The question that runs through the novel—and which plagues Carryl Cope—is Why? Why did Jane do it? A cold and fractured home life clearly did Jane little good, but Carryl Cope, to her credit, is unwilling to explain away Jane's plagiarism on that count alone. For two years Jane had been Carryl's prize student—the singular, exceptional student, the one in a thousand, the "brilliant mind . . .[with] that extra dimension of passionate interest." Watching Jane learn, Carryl tells Lucy, was "intoxicating . . . like watching bamboo grow a yard a night" (p. 124). And yet there is the plagiarism. Despite all of this intellectual growth, did Carryl somehow fail Jane as a teacher?

This question finds no definitive answer until the penultimate scene of the novel. There, Jennifer Finch (a senior faculty member who is something of the resident sage) tells Carryl that for all the time, for all the books, and for all the learning she has given to Jane, she has nonetheless withheld a "crucial," an "essential" element—namely, love (p. 239).

Carryl withheld love not because she didn't feel it, but because she was afraid. She was afraid of the exposure, the risk, and the vulnerability that it entailed. After all, what if the teacher reveals a more personal side of herself to a beloved student and the student is singularly unimpressed or, worse still, finds the professor vaguely ludicrous? How much safer to retreat into the accustomed role of revered professor and respected intellectual taskmaster! So Carryl gave Jane extra books upon books and work upon work, when what Jane wanted was some contact—some communion—with Carryl the human being, not just Professor Cope. She wanted to jump the wall, to remove the third entity of the subject matter that stood between them. Carryl's failure was a failure to recognize this. Or perhaps it is better to say that because of her own fear of lowering the wall, Carryl could not recognize Jane's desire to do as much. For her part, Jane worked ever harder and excelled ever more in hope of winning that communion. In return, she found herself facing an ever higher wall of more books and more work.

Jane's desire for contact with Carryl is neither inappropriate nor importunate. After all, she plans to follow in Carryl's footsteps: she wants to go to graduate school and become a professor of medieval history. It is reasonable for her to want a glimpse of Carryl Cope the human being to know what kind of person such a life will yield. It is equally reasonable, if a person has had such a profound effect on one's life (and especially a young life in the making), to want some measure of communion with that person herself.

Breaching this wall is a risky venture for both teacher and student. But if a teacher seeks the good of the student for the student's own sake, if a teacher is to care for the *soul* of the student, then it is a necessary venture. It is a task that Lucy herself undertakes with Pippa Brentwood.

Pippa, in *her* experiment in self-revelation, lingers after Lucy's first class and with tears in her eyes begins to blurt out her personal grief: her father died suddenly over the summer. Before she can get beyond a sentence, however, Lucy, exhausted and unsure of herself, expresses her rather formal condolences and beats a hasty retreat. During a tutorial later in the semester, Pippa again confesses her woe. This time Lucy forces herself to listen. After some time, Lucy manages to console Pippa, but warns her that their meetings must hereafter be on "professional matters." When Pippa expresses dismay, Lucy says that she cannot play the role of "father confessor and friend," protests that she "doesn't believe in college teachers being amateur psychoanalysts," and insists that there must be "an impersonal subject" between them. To all of which Pippa responds by saying that she will come by on personal matters only if she gets "desperate" (pp. 50–51).

Lucy's concerns are legitimate here. Professors aren't trained as psychological counselors, and Appleton—which is currently embroiled in a controversy over whether to employ a full-time psychiatrist (remember, it is the early 1960s)—would do well to hire one. And yet Lucy has enough self-scrutiny not to leave it at that. She wonders whether she has a right to protect herself in such a situation. Is she acting out of selfishness, fatigue, or an unwillingness to give away anything of her inmost heart? If she really believes in helping half-formed persons to become whole, should she withhold herself in such a situation?

Pippa does come back, but not to discuss her late father. She shows up at Lucy's office late one night to discuss Jane Seaman. Like most other students on campus, she has heard of Jane's plagiarism. Like most, she is outraged at the administration's and Carryl Cope's efforts to cover it up and avoid the normal channels of student-administered justice. Lucy, feeling affection for both Carryl and Jane and aware of the pain and complexity involved, slowly begins to discuss the affair openly and earnestly with Pippa.

"The walls have fallen," she thinks to herself, but rather than regretting that, she comes to see that their increased intimacy is based on mutual respect (p. 136). By the end of the talk, both Lucy's and Pippa's views of the situation have been enlarged, and as the two part they shake hands warmly—like two human beings for a change," Lucy thinks. Alone again in her office, Lucy finds herself wondering whether it is during such crises and in the intimacy they engender that real education flourishes (p. 138).

Interestingly enough, Pippa is doing excellent academic work by the end of the semester. "You taught me a lot," she tells Lucy. But she adds that doing it for Lucy, and not just any professor, gave her "an extra edge." When Lucy protests that Pippa should do her good work for herself, Pippa is adamant. She worked this hard for Lucy, as well as for herself. "Teaching is more than just a subject," she tells Lucy. "It's a person, too. You can't get away from that, even if you want to" (p. 212).

Conclusion

Carryl Cope's ethical failure is an excessive and self-willed distance from Jane outside the classroom. Lucy's ethical success, almost despite herself, is that she manages to strike the right kind of relationship outside the classroom with both Jane and Pippa. What motivates Lucy is a kind of compassion: she cares about each, and she finds herself cautiously and with much uncertainty trying to do what is best for them. Of course, student-teacher contact outside the classroom should not be limited to personal or campus crises. Sometimes, the student simply needs to discuss job, vocation, or graduate school possibilities. As Lucy herself discovers, sometimes even the perfunctory social event (less likely to be a tea these days) has its moments. The key ethical point, however, is that the professor—both inside and outside the classroom—should act as a friend.

This does not mean (at least with my expanded meaning of friendship) that the professor plays favorites or "hangs out" with students. It does mean, however, that the professor brings passion to her subject, and gives of herself for the students' good. With such passionate self-giving, the professor acts as a friend to the students through the medium of the subject matter. This *mediated intimacy* best describes the student-teacher friendship in the classroom. As for relations outside the classroom, sometimes they too are mediated by the subject matter—when a student comes by the office to discuss an assigned reading or paper, for example. At other times, however, they can and should move beyond the subject matter. But here too the professor should always act as a friend, seeking the good of the student for the student's own sake.

I cannot lay down rules about how to act for the student's good in every conceivable situation. Whether a professor should counsel a student or direct him to psychological services, when a professor should seek out the seemingly troubled student, or when she should seek some distance from the unduly importunate student—these and similar questions must be left to the good judgment of the professor. (*The Small Room* does provide some excellent models to inform such judgments.) Nevertheless, I venture this much: to ascertain the ethics of the student-teacher relationship, we must first recognize it as a unique kind of friendship.

References

Aristotle. *Nicomachean Ethics.* (M. Oswald, trans.) Indianapolis, Ind.: Bobbs-Merrill, 1962.

Cahn, S. M. *Saints and Scamps: Ethics in Academia.* Totowa, N.J.: Rowman & Littlefield, 1986.

Markie, P. J. *A Professor's Duties.* Lanham, Md.: Rowman & Littlefield, 1994.

Nussbaum, M. "Literature and Ethics." In L. C. Becker and C. B. Becker (eds.) *Encyclopedia of Ethics.* New York: Garland, 1992.

Sarton, M. *The Small Room.* New York: W. W. Norton, 1961.

Sibley, A. *May Sarton.* New York: Twayne, 1972.

RICHARD L. BAKER, JR., *is associate professor of philosophy and director of the Knight Program in Applied Ethics at Presbyterian College.*

*Advocacy may be unavoidable, but this tendency does not license use
of classrooms as platforms for partisan persuasion. Teaching governed
by fundamental academic virtues will responsibly call students to
genuine, fruitful engagement with political and ethical issues.*

Between Apathy and Advocacy: Teaching and Modeling Ethical Reflection

Karen Hanson

Should college teachers disclose their ethical or political commitments in the
context of student instruction? A good answer requires more than the vague
idea that course content should match course description and the assumption
that course objectives are suitably constrained by the dictates of a teacher's discipline or the course's place in a larger curriculum.

While these general notions of academic appropriateness and professional
responsibilities may be enough to tell us that the physics teacher who uses a
course on quantum mechanics to argue for gay rights legislation has stepped
out of bounds, the contours of relevant discussion are not always so prominently defined. (Moreover, stepping out of bounds may not always be a moral
mistake. Whether otherwise irrelevant discussion is justifiable depends on the
details, the context, and the extremity of the case.) Even what counts as an ethical or political commitment—or what will count for some students as such—
is not always clear. The psychologist who dispassionately discusses human
homosexuality in a course on sexuality or the biologist who presents evolutionary theories to explain the variety of life forms may be unpleasantly surprised by complaints about moral laxity and political bias.

What, if anything, should be done to obviate these sorts of complaints?
And how do our thoughts about such cases illuminate the more patently problematic cases in courses where politics and moral commitments form the very
substance of the syllabus?

Courses focused on contemporary moral controversies present obvious
opportunities for professorial self-revelation and even proselytizing. In a political

science course on national health care policy, for example, the teacher may tend to articulate most fully and forcefully the positions he or she finds most compelling. Or in a philosophy course on applied ethics—one with sections on abortion, euthanasia, the death penalty, and the justifiability of race-based hiring or admissions—the teacher could take *as an educational duty* the controlling aim of helping students see the cogency of the positions he or she judges *correct*.

Even when there is a careful attempt to proceed as if from a point of neutrality, when required readings are scrupulously "balanced" and when equal time is devoted to the exposition of the best arguments for and against all leading contentions in the debate, the professor may find that students become curious about which side is in fact embraced by an "authority" who can apparently survey the entire field clearly. Indeed, by keeping his or her opinions cloaked, the teacher may sometimes make those opinions more intriguing, so that students become perversely focused not on grasping a range of argumentation but on solving the particular and personal enigma of the professor's private opinion.

Students thus may be inappropriately distracted from the crucial business at hand if they find sufficiently interesting the guise of impartiality or the teacher who wears it. Another danger, though, is that apparent neutrality may be profoundly uninteresting. Perhaps only open advocacy, or at least self-disclosure, reveals the seriousness of moral and political issues and thereby helps engage students. Teachers who claim not to reveal their own views in the classroom are, according to some critics, either subtle seducers who draw in fresh converts with an air of mystery, or ineffective stiffs who leave students cold by keeping the heat of controversy at a distance. The methodically neutral teacher may not only bore students but may also unwittingly contribute to cynicism or thoughtless relativism, because students deprived of seeing commitment may well come to view moral and political controversies as merely academic debates, where form counts for much but any position is, at base, as good as any other.

Defenders of neutrality can make mirror-image criticisms of open advocacy: it is pathological narcissism to suppose that the professor, and his or her particular morals or politics, should serve as the focus of a course. If it is not arrogance or self-love that provokes self-display, then it is a thoughtless abuse of authority or power. Moreover it is not, in the end, true engagement that professorial proselytizing will provoke. A clear declaration of the teacher's position on a contested issue is more likely to short-circuit students' wrestling with the issue, because students sense that they have now been given what is, in one way or another, the "right" answer. Students may then mouth—for one semester—the views the professor holds dear, but that may be because they are waiting for their grades. If they actually do become zealous converts, their views will be held on faith, not grounded on objective evidence and reason, because they will have been deliberately deprived of a context of objective study.

The potential problems may seem equally balanced so that the debate appears to be a draw, but critics of neutrality routinely play a trump: keeping one's personal views out of the course is in fact impossible. Teachers who believe they keep their own views out of the classroom are, these critics contend, simply self-deceived. Course design is inherently an exercise in selectivity. Which topics, which texts, which questions—these matters and more are largely decided by an instructor's view of things. A teacher may strive for balance, but the very idea of appropriate balance is perspectival. No professor can seriously aim for a God's-eye view of the subject, a position from which "the whole picture" can be truly and dispassionately surveyed.

These claims about selectivity and perspective are surely correct, but properly understood they do little to help the case of those who would put their personal agenda on the course syllabus. After all, it does not follow from the inevitability of selection that selection must be aimed at producing acolytes. Even if teachers must constantly make choices—from the shape of an assignment to the direction of a discussion—it does not follow that these choices must always tend toward the revelation or promulgation of their particular ethical or political judgments.

From the chimerical nature of the idea of a "complete" survey of a controversy we certainly cannot infer the appropriateness of directing students—implicitly or explicitly—to endorse the teacher's favored point of view. The teacher who aims for balanced readings, who tries to inhabit a variety of viewpoints in lecture and discussion, may not mistakenly believe that the students have thereby been given all possible sides to an argument, all possible interpretations of events. The teacher may believe, correctly, that these methods help students to recognize and negotiate the partiality of perspectives and to develop broad sympathies and informed, independent thought. This, the professor may believe, is a fundamental point of ethics courses.

Furthermore, there is really no reason to suppose that teaching techniques defined in opposition to proselytization are especially likely to promote boredom or disengagement. All good teachers are advocates in some ways. There is even an etymological link between being a professor—one who speaks or avows publicly—and being an advocate—one who calls or speaks to others, summoning their support. The teacher who tries to make the best case for a *variety* of positions may, in the end, possess a deeper and more defensible sense of professorial advocacy than the tendentious teacher.

Engagement with issues can be *shown* as well as declared, after all. Teachers who can nimbly convey the strengths of a position they in fact oppose, who can clearly display weaknesses in a position they in fact embrace, are *modeling* a critical engagement from which students may learn their most important lessons. It is not apathy but vigorous thought and sensitivity that are displayed, even as the explicit marking of the positions the teacher happens to hold is put aside as irrelevant. Such a teacher can embody reflection, and it is clear that such reflection proceeds from an abundance of feelings (some of them in conflict) and from an excess of plausible ideas (some of them contradicting others). Sorting through those feelings and ideas, delineating the reasons and passions that support various views, the teacher can let his or her actual personality and choices become irrelevant. This teacher becomes not authoritative but *exemplary,* an advocate for *thought* who summons students to support and to continue *this* activity, critical thinking, on their own. This teacher is thus tendentious, but the aim is one that all academics must endorse: encouraging and empowering critical thought.

The rationale for this approach to the most problematic parts of the curriculum, the courses in which ethics and politics are the central topics, is equally pertinent to the subtler cases, circumstances in which moral and political questions erupt on a topic the professor might have supposed quite uncontroversial. This salience is perhaps surprising, because with some subjects, in some fields, it does not make sense to think that the professor should put aside the substantive commitments of the field or screen from students his or her allegiance to specific doctrines. For example, the biologist accounting for the variety of life forms should certainly not be expected to shelve or screen his or her full commitment to evolutionary theory.

But suppose a student objects, complaining that evolutionary theory is just one opinion and creationism is an alternative more respectful of the dignity of humanity. Will education be served if the teacher here simply reiterates his or her own commitment to modern biology, if there is an immediate appeal to the authority of the discipline or to the professor's standing within it? The conscientious teacher will serve the student better—and at the same time better serve the discipline—by taking seriously a sincere challenge, trying to understand its ground, and then *showing* the strong and the weak points of both the challenge and the scientific view. This could sometimes seem a distraction from the course material, but the teacher may well find that it is only through these sorts of ruminations that the objecting student—and perhaps the whole class—can really be brought to a deeper understanding of *science.* The practice of reflection that enables noncoercive instruction in ethics and politics does shift the discussion to a metalevel here, but that should not be ruled out of bounds. Students thinking about the *nature* of science are still surely thinking about science.

Students and their professors must employ in this reflective practice some of the central virtues of academia: openness to ideas, honesty in their evaluations, courtesy, and civil respect. That this method of teaching requires embracing the institution's defining values may count as one more point in its favor. In difficult circumstances, our allegiance to these values may not be enough to ensure the moral or pedagogical adequacy of our behavior. But we will surely not do well if those values and the practices they support are abandoned.

KAREN HANSON *is professor of philosophy and a Poynter Fellow at Indiana University. She is writing a book on curricular controversies for Rowman & Littlefield's series* Issues in Academic Ethics.

This chapter reviews faculty members' responsible practices in ensuring fairness, as well as the essential role of staff members and administrators in creating and enhancing a climate of fairness throughout the institution.

Institutional Commitment to Fairness in College Teaching

Rita Cobb Rodabaugh

What Is Fairness and Why Is It Important?

Think back to the very worst experiences you had as a student or to your poorest teachers. As you recall these experiences, the word *unfair* is likely to come to mind. Unfairness commonly describes unsatisfactory educational experiences and poor teachers. On the other hand, *fairness* is invariably a primary factor used by students to describe the "best" teachers they encountered during their educational experiences.

Ethical dimensions of college and university teaching require that we consider fairness as a preeminent objective of the educational process. Just as people expect fairness in business, in the courts, in government, and on the job, college students expect fairness in their courses. We must maintain fairness, not just because it is expected, but because failing to do so has dire consequences for students. Lack of fairness is related to poor achievement, to attrition, and even to campus vandalism (DeMore, Fisher, and Baron, 1988), while maintaining fairness both increases students' satisfaction with the institution (Rodabaugh, 1994) and increases achievement (Marsh and Overall, 1980).

Colleges and universities should institutionalize fairness because the very nature of higher education demands it. Society rests upon the rules of law that foster and maintain civilization, and certainly higher education should epitomize a civilized society. The decisions of the Supreme Court are accepted by most people as legitimate, in large part because the Supreme Court is believed to uphold higher standards than other segments of society. Likewise, colleges and universities should embody ideals and principles that place them above the materialism and vulgarity of a lesser realm. Traditionally, faculty members and administrators of such institutions have been expected to seek the truth as part of a reasoned approach to human existence.

College courses represent, perhaps, the first opportunity most students will have to experience the world as independent adults. This is true even for many returning older students who feel that for the first time in their lives they are finally doing something for themselves rather than doing only what others expect of them. For many students, regardless of age, the college community will become the reference group against which they establish certain values and ideals that will be maintained throughout their lives (Newcomb, 1943; 1967). Indeed, many students even accept the college or university as a model for the ethical dimensions of their lives. This is not a responsibility that faculty members and administrators should take lightly.

Fairness on the college campus cannot be a concern merely of faculty members; it must also fall within the purview of administrators and staff members. The total climate of any organization is established and maintained in accordance with the cumulative behaviors of all members of that organization. But the role of those who hold power and authority is much greater in terms of the impact on the employees and the total constituencies of their organizations. On the college campus, the power and authority vested in administrators means that the potential impact of their behaviors is critical to the promotion of fairness. Faculty members can follow the rules of fairness in the classroom, but administrators must accept the responsibility for establishing an environment within which fairness can be institutionalized.

Research on fairness has shown that people in general expect fairness in their interpersonal relationships (Bies and Moag, 1986), in the distribution of valued resources (Adams, 1965), and in the rules that are employed to determine the distribution of valued resources (McClintock and Van Avermaet, 1982). These three expectations regarding fairness are categorized, respectively, as interactional fairness, outcome fairness, and procedural fairness. In college courses, interactional fairness refers to the relationship between the students and their professors. Outcome fairness refers to the distribution of grades. Procedural fairness refers not only to the rules and regulations that are employed to determine grades, but also to policies regarding attendance, make-up tests, cheating and plagiarism, and other student performance.

How Students View Fairness

In order to create a classroom climate considered by college students to be fair, we must understand what "fairness" means to them. Students are concerned with interactional fairness, procedural fairness, and outcome fairness, in that order. According to college students, the most serious offense that can be committed by faculty members is showing partiality to some students on the basis of gender, race, or age. Other violations of interactional fairness that students resent are: being "angry" or "mean" in class (including using profanity, yelling, or screaming); embarrassing students in the classroom, especially by using sarcasm and put-downs; exhibiting an uncaring attitude toward students; and failing to respond to student questions (Rodabaugh, 1994).

Procedural fairness is considered to be more important than outcome fairness because students, like the general population, assume that if the procedures for determining outcomes are fair, then the outcomes will be fair. This means that students rate a "tough" faculty member (one who is very strict and gives low grades, but is scrupulously fair) as more caring, worthy of respect, likeable, and appealing than a professor who is very lax and gives high grades, but is not always evenhanded with students (Rodabaugh and Kravitz, 1994).

Student concerns with procedural fairness are clear and straightforward: students expect rules and regulations related to the classroom to be fair to all students, without exceptions. Students also expect tests to be fair and to measure accurately what they have been asked to learn, without trick questions or vague references. They want tests returned promptly and discussed in class, the answers explained, and time allotted for questions. Students are deeply concerned about procedural fairness relative to the monitoring and regulation of cheating and plagiarism.

Adherence to fair outcomes in the classroom dictates that grades reflect fairly student contributions to the class as demonstrated by test scores or the completion of other course requirements. This assumption also applies to individual contributions to group work or cooperative learning assignments. A major point to remember in this connection is that college students expect individual accomplishments to count toward their final grades. Faculty members who consider individual effort when calculating final grades are considered to be fair, while those who "make allowances" (especially for students who exerted little effort or made almost no contribution to the class) are considered to be unfair. The latter are not likely to be selected as professors when students are given a choice (Rodabaugh and Kravitz, 1994).

Students expect a class to be challenging and want the results to discriminate between the various levels of contribution by class members. When most students make A's in an unchallenging class, they consider it to be unfair because input does not match output and no distinction is made between those who worked hard and those who did not.

Faculty's Role in Creating Fairness

Whether or not students look upon their academic experiences as being fair depends largely upon the actions of individual faculty members. If college students view most of their professors as being fair, they will tend to be satisfied with their college experiences. When students believe that most of their professors have been unfair, they display a high level of dissatisfaction with college, and their academic performance often suffers. Faculty members can ensure that their students will perceive them to be fair by adhering to the tenets of interactional, outcome, and procedural fairness.

Interactional Fairness. If faculty members are to follow the dictates of interactional fairness, they must be equally concerned about all students in their classrooms without showing any partiality when answering their questions, when giving them assistance, and when responding through body language or otherwise. Students usually notice any subtle differences related to interactional fairness in faculty behaviors affecting students. These behaviors can affect not only the target student but other students who witness the incident and conclude that the environment is unfair. Faculty members must also go beyond impartiality by showing concern for all students and treating them with respect. Not only does this include being concerned about students, but also *demonstrating* this concern in a number of ways related to interactional fairness. For example, faculty members can demonstrate their respect for students by acting on a sincere concern that they learn the material and by keeping in mind that it is the faculty member's duty to aid students in the learning process.

Most students respect their professors and want to be treated with a similar degree of respect by them. Key aspects of a respectful environment include giving students ample time to ask questions, allowing them to challenge the professor's conclusions without recrimination, and debating or discussing pertinent matters—all politely and accurately, without put-downs or sarcasm. The manner in which student queries are answered or class policies are enforced can make all the difference as to whether a faculty member is thought to be fair. Faculty members should monitor their tone of voice, facial expressions, and body language to be certain that the message being conveyed is not one of sarcasm or indifference, but rather one of respect, concern, fairness, and equality.

In addition to respect, fair practice dictates that interactions involve truthfulness, justification, and propriety (Bies and Moag, 1986). To meet these requirements in the classroom, faculty members must be honest with students in all respects, including saying "I don't know" when appropriate, being straightforward about policies and procedures, and following through with promised consequences (especially the punishment for cheating). Justification practices applicable to the classroom require that faculty members and other institutional representatives explain and justify rules, procedures, and even curricular content. Faculty members should have ready answers for all student queries about such matters. For example, faculty justification might include the statement that attendance is required because attendance is related to student achievement.

Rules of interactional fairness related to basic propriety include respecting students' privacy and using appropriate language. At times, some faculty members pepper their lectures with profanity and vulgarities that many students, perhaps less liberal than their professors, find offensive. Basic propriety calls for a higher tone in the classroom, including maintaining a status differential. Most college students are uncomfortable when relationships between faculty members and students become too friendly. Students generally admire faculty members, but they do not expect to be best friends with them. An especially serious impropriety occurs when a faculty member dates or becomes romantically involved with a student.

Procedural Fairness. Several teaching practices that promote procedural fairness can be introduced easily in college courses. A matter of the utmost importance is the method used for administering tests. When a test is returned promptly so that students can readily see what they missed and ask pertinent questions, then the test becomes a learning and teaching tool, not just a means for assigning grades. When faculty members have reviewed test results and prepared themselves for anticipated student questions before returning the test, they are prepared to state which questions might be disqualified due to ambiguity or which ones have more than one possible response. For some frequently missed questions, the relevant information might be reiterated and even included again on the next test. When handled effectively, the process takes only fifteen to twenty minutes of class time per test, even for a class of 150 students. This small investment of time yields worthwhile results related to student perceptions of fairness and to student learning.

A second important procedural requirement is the establishment and enforcement of rules and regulations regarding attendance. Even if no credit is given for attendance and no points are deducted for absences, monitoring those present each day still increases attendance. Students tend to think that anything that is inspected must be expected, and monitoring attendance simply tells them that the professor thinks attendance is important. Attendance is increased even more if the faculty member explains why attendance is important. For example, some information given in class will not be found in the textbook, and faculty members or administrators often view attendance as one relevant piece of evidence for ascertaining contribution and effort when they assess student performance or consider student problems.

Other rules and regulations that contribute to a fair atmosphere include those related to cheating and plagiarism. Perhaps as many as 90 percent of students in a college class will have cheated at least in some fashion during their college career. Sometimes students "cheat" because they do not consider the behavior in question to be cheating. Some students see nothing amiss in looking at another student's paper to check a few answers. Few students understand plagiarism, and many of them think that changing a few words of a copied piece of information negates any charge of plagiarism.

Faculty members can reduce cheating by implementing a few strategies relative to procedural fairness: discussing the importance of academic honesty, outlining the penalties for cheating, and monitoring course activities in a way designed to eliminate cheating. Faculty members who clearly explain the behaviors that constitute cheating and plagiarism and the penalties for these behaviors encounter fewer instances of each in their classes.

An additional fairness rule that applies to both interactional and procedural fairness relates to what social psychologists call *voice* (Bies and Shapiro, 1986; Folger, Rosenfield, Grove, and Corkran, 1979). Voice is defined as the opportunity to express one's opinion concerning the rules and procedures that are used to determine outcomes. When used in the classroom, voice becomes a powerful force for improving student perceptions of fairness. The process can be as simple as allowing time for questions when distributing course requirements or as complex as giving students some real choice with respect to course requirements.

Small Group Instructional Diagnosis, a process developed by Joseph Clark (Redmond and Clark, 1982), is a particularly effective way of allowing students voice early in a term. With the course instructor out of the room, an outside person conducts a brief survey of students: what is going well? What might be improved? How might the improvement be accomplished? Student responses are discussed in small groups, and the consensus (as well as significant dissent) is reported to the consultant, who clarifies and verifies understanding of the information through dialogue with the students. The in-class activity requires about twenty-five minutes. Following the class, the results of the process are reported to the instructor—without reference to individual students, of course. At a subsequent class session, the instructor responds in turn to the students, clarifying matters as appropriate and considering possible modifications in course procedures.

Even in the simplest scenarios, providing for student voice to be heard increases student perceptions of fairness, whether or not anything is changed due to their input.

Outcome Fairness. Outcome fairness is achieved when a course is challenging and students truly earn the grades assigned to them. Faculty members can accomplish this goal by requiring a high level of achievement in order to earn a high final grade based on performance standards that discriminate among levels of ability and effort. Being "too easy" creates a sense of unfairness not only among those few who normally earn "A's," but also among those who realize they unjustly received a high grade. Fair outcomes are assured when faculty members establish and maintain high standards and fair procedures for maintaining those standards.

Institutionalizing the Process

Most faculty members and administrators agree at least in theory on the need to institutionalize impartial treatment of students (and other rules of interactional fairness), but some may object to strict observance of rules and procedures, one of the chief tenets of procedural fairness. These individuals often argue that "in loco parentis" is dead, and that students are adults and should be treated as such. Other faculty members and administrators view this attitude as detrimental to students, because part of the purpose of higher education is to prepare students for the world of employment— "the real world." Most future employers of college students will not permit the uncontrolled or unregulated atmosphere allowed by some faculty members. If the worker or the student knows that no one is monitoring attendance or tardiness and that no repercussions will occur due to missed work hours or class sessions, how many will be present on all occasions? Students often do not perceive the correlations between attendance and grades; only after receiving an unsatisfactory grade do they complain about the lack of an attendance policy.

Departmental Initiatives. If faculty members within a department can reach some agreement concerning the establishment and implementation of classroom policies and procedures, they will improve student perceptions of fairness and help eliminate student noncompliance. One of the reasons students do not adhere to rules and regulations is because they do not believe that they are really mandatory. As a result of educational experiences where lax rules prevailed, students often do not take seriously those professors who say "only three absences are allowed" or "no make-up tests will be given." When a faculty member occasionally enforces rules, students are shocked and likely to complain that "all of my other professors let us take make-ups" or "my other classes allow more than three cuts." Such misunderstandings become especially troublesome when the faculty member bows to the pressure of an obdurate student or an unsupportive administrator and reneges on an established policy. Ideally, the entire institution should be consistent in setting policies and procedures and adhering to them, but if this type of cooperation cannot be achieved, departmental consistency is at least a beginning.

Why do faculty members relent to student pressure? Some do not want to deal with the hassle; some want "to be liked" by their students; some are afraid that they will not receive administrative support; and others are unsure of whether their policies actually are reasonable. But faculty members who are lax do not gain student respect, and they are deemed to be "less caring toward students" than those who are more strict (Rodabaugh, 1994). Just as it is unlikely that a student has ever complained to a faculty member that more work should be required, it is also unlikely that a student will complain about the laxness of the prevailing rules and regulations. Only after completing a course do students complain about its "easiness" or "permissiveness," often by stating that they "learned nothing" or that it was "unfair."

Role of Administrators. The need for fairness in the college classroom is viewed by students and professors as more important than it is by administrators (Wotruba and Wright, 1975). Even though the actions of faculty members constitute the most important aspects of a fair climate, fairness will not become institutionalized unless administrators understand it, support it, and reward those faculty members who make fairness a priority. Department chairs, deans, and presidents can work together to proclaim fairness as an institutional goal.

Administrators must also support faculty members who monitor their students in order to curb cheating. One of the main reasons given by faculty members for "looking the other way" relative to cheating is that they do not get enough administrative support for enforcing strict regulations. Even though a cheating case is cumbersome and potentially litigious, to look the other way raises serious implications regarding student perceptions of fairness, their satisfaction with college, the level of student performance, and the overall quality of the institution.

Administrators who recognize their role in establishing and maintaining a fair campus climate can also act upon this responsibility in other ways that will increase the effectiveness of the institution. While encouraging fairness among faculty and students, administrators must remember to use the rules of interactional, procedural, and outcome fairness in their own relationships with faculty and staff members. When fairness prevails at an institution, the college community will benefit from a greater sense of harmony, trust, increased job satisfaction, reduced turnover, and lower burnout (Alexander and Ruderman, 1987).

A key area on which administrators should focus is the methodology by which disputes on campus are resolved. In most instances, administrators can monitor dispute resolution policies on campus and assure that the guidelines for fairness are followed—especially by giving all participants a chance to contribute significantly to the proceedings (voice) and to explain their actions (justification). Administrators can assess the commitment to fairness on their campus by examining all relevant policies and procedures. How many questions on the current student evaluation form relate to fairness? When interviewing potential faculty members, how many questions are asked that relate to the candidate's knowledge and concern for fairness?

Conclusion

College students are more concerned with fairness in their courses than with easy grades or brilliant lectures. Students do not mind strict rules so long as the rules are fair and administered equally. Students will even accept faculty members who give a heavy work load and difficult tests if the faculty members are fair. If an institution is concerned with fairness, this commitment can be reflected in the mission statement or in the goals of the institution. Administrators, faculty members, and even trustees can thereby make public their commitment to fairness for all students and to the best possible educational environment.

When the institution upholds fairness in as many ways as possible, students receive the message that the world can be, and should be, a fair place. The world is not always fair, of course, but colleges should be in the business of demonstrating to students that the ideal of fairness can be an organizing principle for social groups and institutions. Given a steady dose of fairness for four years or more, students just might enter society with a heightened commitment to a just social order.

References

Adams, J. S. "Inequity in Social Exchange." In L. Berkowitz (ed.), *Advances in Experimental Social Psychology*. Vol. II. New York: Academic Press, 1965.

Alexander, S., and Ruderman, M. "The Role of Procedural and Distributive Justice in Organizational Behavior." *Social Justice Research,* 1987, *1,* 177–198.

Bies, R. J., and Moag, J. S. "Interactional Justice: Communication Criteria of Fairness." In R. J. Lewicki, B. H. Sheppard, and M. H. Bazerman (eds.), *Research on Negotiation in Organizations.* Vol. I. Greenwich, Conn.: JAI Press, 1986.

Bies, R. J., and Shapiro, D. L. "Voice and Justification: Their Influence on Procedural Fairness Judgments." *Academy of Management Journal,* 1988, *31,* 676–685.

DeMore, S. W., Fisher, J. D., and Baron, R. M. "The Equity-Control Model as a Predictor of Vandalism Among College Students." *Journal of Applied Social Psychology,* 1988, *18,* 80–91.

Folger, R., Rosenfield, D., Grove, J., and Corkran, L. "Effects of 'Voice' and Peer Opinions on Responses to Inequity." *Journal of Personality and Social Psychology,* 1979, *37,* 2253–2261.

Marsh, H. W., and Overall, J. U. "Validity of Students' Evaluations of Teaching Effectiveness: Cognitive and Affective Criteria." *Journal of Educational Psychology,* 1980, *72,* 468–475.

McClintock, C. G., and Van Avermaet, E. "Social Values and Rules of Fairness: A Theoretical Perspective." In V. J. Derlega and J. Grzelak, (eds.), *Cooperation and Helping Behavior: Theories and Research.* New York: Academic Press, 1982.

Newcomb, T. M. *Personality and Social Change: Attitude Formation in a Student Community.* New York: Dryden Press, 1943.

Newcomb, T. M. *Persistence and Change: Bennington College and Its Students After 25 Years.* New York: Wiley, 1967.

Redmond, M. V., and Clark, D. J. "Small Group Instructional Diagnosis: A Practical Approach to Improving Teaching." *AAHE Bulletin,* Feb. 1982, 8–10.

Rodabaugh, R. C. "College Students' Perceptions of Unfairness in the Classroom." *To Improve the Academy,* 1994, *13,* 269–282.

Rodabaugh, R. C., and Kravitz, D. A. "Effects of Procedural Fairness on Student Judgments of Professors." *Journal on Excellence in College Teaching,* 1994, *5* (2), 67–84.

Wotruba, T. R., and Wright, P. L. "How to Develop a Teacher-Rating Instrument." *Journal of Higher Education,* 1975, *46,* 653–663.

RITA COBB RODABAUGH *is dean of social sciences at Ocean County College.*

*This chapter offers practical differentiations among the meanings of
certain terms central to the modern-day ethics dialogue. Clarity in
communication not only can reduce unnecessary and nonproductive
disputation but also can lead to developing appropriately ethical
campus climates.*

Differentiating the Related Concepts of Ethics, Morality, Law, and Justice

Terry T. Ray

Ethics is one of the hottest topics in higher education today. The dialogue in
the academy, however, suffers from a common problem found in many other
fields where the ethics debate is raging: a confusing merger of some of the central terms in usage, often making meaningful dialogue difficult.

Sometime during the decade of the 1980s a general perception emerged
that the United States was undergoing an ethics crisis. Some say it began with
Watergate; others go back to the Vietnam War credibility gap. Regardless, at
some point during the past decade, it came to appear to a critical mass of the
American public that the general ethical behavior of its society had degener-
ated and had become considerably less desirable than it once was. In reaction
to this perceived crisis, there came a public call to fix the problem.

Prior to this tacitly declared "crisis," ethics as a topic of significance had
been primarily confined to the cloistered chambers of university philosophy
departments. With the call to action, however, others took up the mantle and
formed a new class of "ethics operatives," many of whom were not trained ethi-
cists. Soon, a wide variety of individuals from many disciplines and professions
were into the fray, expounding their own personal views on ethics and providing popular forums and special programs on the subject—from Donahue
to Dan Quayle, from CBS to PBS. With this grass-roots ethics phenomenon
came a certain layman's laxity in terminology. The meaning of the term *ethics*
was substantially broadened to include many concepts quite beyond its classical definition. This terminological expansion substantially contributed to the
problem mentioned in the opening paragraph. With the resulting lack of a
working definitional consensus on central terms in the modern ethics dialogue,
meaningful exchange has often become difficult.

New Directions for Teaching and Learning, no. 66, Summer 1996 © Jossey-Bass Publishers

The purpose of this chapter is to suggest some practical differentiations among the meanings of certain terms central to the modern ethics dialogue—*ethics, morality, law,* and *justice*—particularly as they are used in the context of teaching in the college and university setting. Along with working definitions, suggestions are also offered on how to untangle many of the common terminological knots encountered in the college and university ethics dialogue on teaching.

Defining *Ethics*

The common and traditional definition of ethics is: a branch of philosophy comprising various moralistic models or schools of thought designed to bring about "good" within a society. Two examples of classic ethical models are Utilitarianism and Kantianism. Each of these schools of ethical thought sets forth differing rationales for determining ethicality. With different frames of reference, different conclusions are often reached among ethics models as to the ethicality of a given circumstance. What is ethical for one may be unethical for another.

According to the principles of the Utilitarian school of ethics, an act is ethical if it brings about the greatest good to the greatest number of people—for example, using a teaching method that benefits the greatest number of students in a classroom, not adjusting downward for a minority of slower individuals. On the other hand, the Kantian model holds that in an ethical society, certain rights of the individual (free consent, privacy, free conscience, free speech, due process) should not be violated regardless of other good intentions—for example, allowing an irate student to vent her point of view in a classroom, even though it impedes the progress of the majority of other students. It is easy to see how a Kantian and a Utilitarian could very well disagree on the ethicality of a given situation.

In the modern era, many institutions and professions have broadened the classical meaning of *ethics* by applying the term to adopted principles or rules of organizational conduct, often referred to as an ethics code. With this usage of the term, ethical conduct has come to be determined by an often quasi-legalistic application of code provisions to the conduct under consideration. Some of these codes maintain a traditional, moralistic, philosophical bent; others are much more practical, specific, and regulatory. Given the nature of these latter codes, one can reasonably question whether they are in essence law or ethics (a differentiation to be examined later in this chapter). Classical ethics and code ethics are somewhat different; the former is a comprehensive philosophy of "good" conduct, the latter is more rule-oriented and less philosophical. They are similar in that both set a desired norm for conduct in a social entity: general society for the former, organizational context for the latter.

The most pervasive terminological problem regarding the use of the term *ethics* is the tendency of many to use *unethical* for virtually any behavior that is deemed unacceptable, although the concept in mind may be something other than ethics. From a practical point of view, one may ask, does this terminological inaccuracy really matter? Is it really significant if one uses *ethics* for describing conduct deemed undesirable, instead of *morality, law,* or *justice?*

Having been a party to a great many ethics dialogues over the last decade, this writer can respond that it clearly does matter. It matters because terminological inaccuracy impedes a true meeting of the minds. The use of a term, if its meaning to the listener is not the same as that intended by the speaker, can (and often does) create unnecessary disagreement among the parties and spawn frustrating monological detours as well. This writer has found that if terminological consensus can be reached at the initiation of an ethics dialogue, far less acrimony and frustration are likely to be encountered and far more productive exchange and meaningful closure can be anticipated.

Defining *Morality*

Morality can be reasonably defined as a belief in right and wrong that is autonomous, self-standing, and not dependent, as with ethics, on a philosophical rationale for validation—for example, "Thou shalt not kill" and "Honesty is the best policy." Morality is also different from ethics in its applicable context. Whereas an ethical goal of righteous conduct is oriented toward a defined social entity—general society or a human organization, for example—a moral is normally held to be of a universal nature and not limited to any particular social entity. The relationship of morality to classical ethics can also be viewed as a component to the aggregate. Metaphorically, if one views ethics as a wall, morals are the building blocks and philosophy is the mortar. Ethics, corresponding to this metaphor, is often described as *moral philosophy.*

We are all familiar with the ancient biblical moral, "Do unto others as you would have others do unto you." This simple moral, set forth as the Golden Rule, has been incorporated and expanded into an ethical philosophy known as the Golden Rule Model—taking the platitudinal nature of the moral and rationally working out its systematic social application to real life. This difference between the essence of a moral belief and an ethical judgment can lead to quite different views on the same matter. Consider, for instance, the opposing views of the death penalty. Those who support it often take a Utilitarian ethics approach: executing any individual may be an unfortunate circumstance, but the net result will be to bring the greatest good to the greatest number of people. A severe penalty, deterrence, and a lower homicide rate are equated. This *ethical* position can be rationally and objectively defended and debated through use of empirical data. On the other hand, opponents of the death penalty tend to adopt a *moral* view of the matter: killing is wrong, regardless of who commits it. This statement of view essentially ends the conversation. It is presented as an accepted universal belief, not offered for rational debate but as a given statement of right and wrong.

A common terminological phenomenon of the modern ethics dialogue in regard to the term *morality* is the tendency to casually interchange the terms *ethics* and *morality,* using them as virtual synonyms. On the surface this tendency may not appear to be significant, but in practice it can be quite important and problematic. The level of emotional commitment and rationality one possesses in regard to a particular view of right and wrong depends on whether it is a moral or ethical view. One who bases a point of view on a morality will be much more likely to have a significantly higher emotional attachment to the position and will be much less likely to submit that position to rational analysis than if the position were based on an ethical standard. This contrast in attitude derives from the differences between the two concepts—morality and ethics. A belief in a morality tends to be of an unquestioning nature—accepting its validity, truth, and righteousness—whereas ethical positions tend to be far more philosophical and rational.

Therefore, in an "ethical" dialogue it is important to reject the false synonymy of morality and ethics and specifically determine whether a participant is basing a position on morality or ethics, despite the chosen term being used. This determination can greatly assist in deciding one's choice of approach to a prospective dialogue. If a participant's position is of a *moral* nature, others may realistically anticipate strong resistance to rational discussion. If, on the other hand, it is *ethically* based, much more success can be anticipated in engaging a rational dialogue. In the academy's ethical dialogue on teaching, as with all other ethical dialogues, it is essential to separate moral positions from ethical positions as soon as possible in order to increase the likelihood of a meaningful exchange of ideas.

Defining *Law*

When the word *law* is used in today's world, it is likely to conjure images of complex legislation, byzantine regulations, and courtroom drama. The true essence of law, however, is much more basic. Law, simply stated, is a means by which human beings maintain control over one another through fear of punishment ("Do as I say or suffer the consequences.") A father telling his teenager to have the car back before midnight or be grounded for two weeks is clearly issuing law. The element of coercion is what distinguishes law from both ethics and morality. Failure to recognize this difference is another conceptual difficulty encountered in the modern ethics dialogue.

When a campus perceives that the incidence of undesirable faculty conduct in the classroom has reached an unacceptable level or when a particularly grievous act shocks the collective conscience of the academic community, a call for reform often issues. Proposed solutions frequently split into two camps: to set clear standards for desired faculty conduct and encourage attainment, or to set clear standards and enforce conformance through use of negative sanctions. Both of these approaches are commonly suggested in connection with the *ethics code.* The divergence of the approaches (though most fail to recognize the nature of the dichotomy) is the gulf between ethical and legal thinking—between positive and negative sanctions to achieve desired ends. Many in such a dialogue call for measures to "straighten out errant faculty," purely a legalistic approach, while consistently and inaccurately using the term *ethics* to describe their approach.

It is important to bring the differences in these concepts into the open in such a dialogue for two reasons. First, it will clarify the positions, each side being able to clearly appreciate the other's thinking and agenda. Second, it will put on the table for examination how the two camps diverge on their views toward non-conformance and will raise the question as to the respective effect on the faculty that each approach may have. Under an ethical system, a faculty member will draw upon both rational powers and personal conscience in conforming to the recommended ethics. Under a legal system, faculty will approach conformance quite differently. When faced with potential punishment for non-conformance, one's basis of decision making shifts dramatically from rationality and conscience to self protection. Under a legal system, one does not tend to see the standards as goals for aspiration but as potential threats to one's well-being.

A college or university community attempting to effect change in faculty classroom conduct should consciously consider the significant differences between a legalistic and an ethical approach to a solution, bearing in mind what effect each system will have on the campus culture. An ethical system sets desirable goals for faculty conduct and, with encouragement, trusts the faculty's goodwill and conscience to aspire toward the mark. A legal system polices faculty conduct and brings about conformance through fear of negative sanctions. These dichotomous approaches, though both effective in changing conduct, produce significantly different campus cultures. When undertaking "ethical" problems, a college or university should deliberately determine what sort of culture it wishes to foster.

A final area of importance relating to the term *law* is the common modern-day practice of *intentionally* merging law with ethics or morality to one's own advantage. When asked if one's questionable actions were unethical or immoral, a not uncommon response in today's world is, "I have acted entirely within the law." This is, of course, unresponsive. A legal standard, as discussed earlier, is distinctly different from an ethical or moral standard. A faculty member, for instance, who places his name alone on a journal article entirely researched and written on his behalf by a graduate assistant may quite correctly state that he has acted entirely within the law (not having violated the copyright law), but this clearly does not equate to having acted ethically or morally. A professor who has unquestionably taken sexual advantage of a student but is able to win the case in court on a highly technical procedural point can accurately say that he has done nothing *illegal,* but that does not mean he has acted ethically or morally. A practical method of dealing with a person who uses this obfuscation technique to escape culpability is to ask the dodger for his definition of terms. Does he believe legality to be synonymous with ethicality and morality, and if so, by what definitions? This technique can often effectively flush out into the open a person using this terminological ruse.

Defining *Justice*

It is not uncommon for an ethics dialoguer to use *justice* as a synonym for ethics, morality, and law—for example, "his actions were just," possibly implying ethical, moral, or legal conduct. As with the other terms discussed earlier, this inappropriate synonymy can be problematic. The following is offered as a working definition of the term: justice is a perception that *fairness* has been achieved by a particular action. This distinguishes justice from the other three concepts; fairness is not necessarily an intrinsic element of ethics, morality, or law.

As an example of justice in application, consider a situation in which a student receives a failing grade for an entire course for plagiarizing a single paragraph of a final paper. He will likely protest the professor's actions as being *unjust*. On the other hand, a student who was suffering from a fever during a final exam and who is allowed to retake it—although the professor stated in class there would be no re-examinations—will likely view the professor's action as *just*. In both circumstances, if the student has based his judgment on an assessment of the professor's fairness under the circumstance, the use of *justice* is in accordance with the suggested working definition. Not everyone, though, uses the term *justice* as separate and distinct from the other central terms under consideration.

Of all the central terms discussed in this chapter, probably *law* is most often inappropriately merged with *justice*. When a particularly noticeable lack of fairness is perceived on a campus, there frequently is a call to promulgate a policy to "ensure justice." If, for instance, a campus is wrestling with what to do about a perception that student classroom cheating is being dealt with in a very inconsistent (and therefore unfair) manner by the faculty, a "Policy on Student Classroom Cheating" is commonly suggested as a remedy. Those who desire to see justice dispensed to students accused of cheating equate achievement of this end with the creation of such a policy. What they fail to realize is that once such a policy is written, a legal system is created and justice—no longer an end nor a consideration—is displaced. To understand this statement, one needs to understand the relationship of justice to law.

It is understandable why justice and law are so often perceived to be inextricably intertwined. Courts are frequently referred to as halls of justice adorned by the ubiquitous presence of Blind Justice with her blindfold and scales. In actual practice, however, once any concept of right and wrong—be it ethics, morality, or justice—is codified it sheds its original nature and takes on a legal nature. Whether enforcement of a cheating code or a murder statute, the legal objective is the same: the correct application of the law to the facts of the case. As anyone who has even a passing knowledge of the operation of a legal system is aware, law correctly applied has no direct correlation to justice, ethics, or morality. As noted by Mr. Bumble in Dickens' *Oliver Twist*, "If the law supposes that, the law is a ass, a idiot." Frequently, people may rue the lack of justice in legally correct judicial decisions. For example, when a vicious murderer is set free by reason of an incorrectly typed search warrant—a correct *legal* ruling—to many it is a clear abandonment of *justice*.

When an institution establishes a policy on cheating and other academic transgressions, decisions under that policy will typically be the responsibility of some designated tribunal. Anyone who has served on such a body knows full well that one's commission in so serving is not to dispense *justice* but to gather the facts of the case and come to a decision by properly applying the relevant provisions of the policy to those facts. One is not free, if properly carrying out one's assigned responsibilities, to disregard the policy and autonomously issue a *just* ruling.

What one needs to take from this explanation of justice and law is that if one attempts to regulate justice, justice itself is lost in the transition. If one truly wishes to see the dispensation of *justice,* one must be willing to trust the unregulated goodwill, common sense, and free conscience of others to do so. If one is not willing to so trust, one must be satisfied with the machine-like nature of legal proceedings. When considering a course of action with "ethical" issues on campus, where justice is an issue one needs to ponder the ultimate effect certain decisions can have on an institutional culture. As in the discussion of ethics codes, a campus community dealing with issues of justice should consciously reflect on its collective view, examining specifically its faith (or lack thereof) in the free will and goodwill of its constituency.

Conclusion

Communication is always imperfect. The best human beings can do is to attempt to express their concepts and ideas in a manner that will allow others to understand at least their fundamental essence. A person who is monolingual in English will understand virtually nothing that a French speaker is attempting to convey for the obvious reason that the words have no meaning. On a limited basis, the same difficulty is encountered by those speaking the same language if they don't understand the meaning of words used by one another or if the words they use mean something different to each of them. Certain issues come upon a society so swiftly, with a corresponding rapid evolution of language, that there is insufficient time to reach consensual clarity on terminology.

As presented in this chapter, this writer perceives the modern dialogue on "ethics" to be just such a case. Given enough time, consensual clarity will eventually emerge. Until then, working definitions of central terms are needed; I have offered them here for the interim.

TERRY T. RAY *is professor and chair of finance and legal studies at Indiana University of Pennsylvania.*

Academic ethics are "academic" in the pejorative sense if not applied in all the activities that make up academic life.

The Ethics of Knowledge

Clark Kerr

The central purposes of academic activity are the discovery of knowledge through research and its dissemination through teaching. Certain ethical rules are inherent in the creation and distribution of knowledge. These ethical principles are rules for guiding judgment about conduct in the intellectual sphere, and they set moral limits to action above those required by law.

The ethics of knowledge has a number of components. These components are the rules of conduct appropriate to the effective advancement of knowledge, and to the integrity of teachers in relations with students and of scholars in their relations with other scholars. They declare, as I understood them, the following actions to be obligatory:

- The careful collection and use of evidence, including the search for "inconvenient facts," as in the process of attempted "falsification."
- The careful use of ideas and the work of others.
- The obligation to be skeptical of what is not fully proven.
- An openness to alternative explanations. This requires full freedom of expression; and this "academic freedom," in turn, requires tolerance of other points of view than one's own.
- Civility in discourse, and reliance on persuasion rather than on coercion.
- Open access to the results of research conducted within the university.
- The reliance on academic merit alone in evaluating the academic performance of others.

This chapter is excerpted from *Higher Education Cannot Escape History: Issues for the Twenty-first Century* (pp. 139–141), by Clark Kerr, 1994. It is reprinted by special permission of the author and the State University of New York Press.

- Care and consideration in handling human and animal subjects so as not to injure them unduly in the process of obtaining knowledge.
- Avoidance of drawing and advancing policy applications unless the full range of considerations entering into policy making has been the subject of study; and unless not only actions, but also possible reactions, have been considered. Scholars should not go beyond their knowledge.
- Separating personal knowledge, based on moral and political values, from the presentation of evidence and analysis; and, as a corollary, making any personal evaluations explicit.
- Following the principle of "fair share," as defined by Rawls (1971, p. 343) and which applies to other organizations in addition to the academic, that "a person is under an obligation to do his part as specified by the rules of an institution whenever he has voluntarily accepted the benefits of the scheme or has taken advantage of the opportunities it offers to advance his interests, provided this institution is just and fair. . . .We are not to gain from the cooperative efforts of others without doing our fair share."
- Rejecting the use of position and facilities made available for the creation and transmission of knowledge for the advancement of unrelated personal pecuniary or political goals or of ideological convictions.
- The full acceptance of the obligations to students to teach them faithfully, to advise them carefully, and to evaluate them fairly, and not to exploit them in any way.
- The full acceptance of the obligation to academic colleagues to assist them with advice on their academic pursuits, and to do so particularly for junior colleagues.
- The full acceptance of the obligation, within departments, to seek a reasonable balance of colleagues by age, by subject matter specialty, and by analytic method.

Academic ethics apply not only to scientific scholarly research, but also to teaching. Academic ethics are "academic" in the pejorative sense if not applied in all the activities that make up academic life.

The validity and pertinence of the obligations that make up academic ethics have even wider applicability. For example, "a respect for evidence and for contrary opinion are qualities of mind that we need throughout the society, as we resist the terrible certainties and brutal simplifications of the fanatic, the doctrinaire, the bigot, and the demagogue" (Trow, 1976, p. 23).

References

Rawls, John. *A Theory of Justice,* Cambridge: Harvard University Press, 1971.
Trow, Martin. "Higher Education and Moral Development," *AAUP Bulletin, 62,* 1976, 20–27.

CLARK KERR is president emeritus of the University of California.

Designing, carrying out, and analyzing instruction requires taking into account certain ethical guidelines, ideals, and expectations.

Ethical Principles for College and University Teaching

Harry Murray, Eileen Gillese, Madeline Lennon, Paul Mercer, Marilyn Robinson

This chapter presents a set of basic ethical principles that define the professional responsibilities of college and university professors in their role as teachers. Ethical principles are conceptualized here as general guidelines, ideals, or expectations that need to be taken into account, along with other relevant conditions and circumstances, in the design and analysis of teaching. This document is not intended to provide a list of ironclad rules or a systematic code of conduct, along with prescribed penalties for infractions, that will automatically apply in all situations and govern all eventualities. Similarly, the intent of this document is not to contradict the concept of academic freedom but rather to describe ways in which academic freedom can be exercised in a responsible manner. Finally, this document is not intended as a final product that is ready for adoption in the absence of thorough discussion and consideration of local needs.

The material that follows was taken from *Ethical Principles in University Teaching,* developed by the Society for Teaching and Learning in Higher Education (STLHE) and to be distributed to university professors across Canada with the support of 3M Canada. The rationale for this document is that in times of increased debate about accountability in higher education, there is a need for a statement that clarifies the duties and responsibilities of teachers. The STLHE believes that a statement of ethical principles in teaching should be written by individuals who are active teachers rather than being handed down by higher authorities.

Portions of this chapter were previously published by the Society for Teaching and Learning in Higher Education and are adapted here by permission.

PRINCIPLE 1: Content Competence
> A university teacher maintains a high level of subject matter knowledge and
> ensures that course content is current, accurate, representative, and appropriate
> to the position of the course within the student's program of studies.

This principle means that a teacher is responsible for maintaining (or acquiring) subject matter competence not only in areas of personal interest but in all areas relevant to course goals or objectives. Appropriateness of course content implies that what is actually taught in the course is consistent with stated course objectives and prepares students adequately for subsequent courses for which the present course is a prerequisite. Representativeness of course content implies that for topics involving difference of opinion or interpretation, representative points of view are acknowledged and placed in perspective.

Achievement of content competence requires that the teacher take active steps to be up-to-date in content areas relevant to his or her courses, to be informed of the content of prerequisite courses and of courses for which the teacher's course is prerequisite, and to provide adequate representation of important topic areas and points of view.

Specific examples of failure to fulfill the principle of content competence occur when an instructor teaches subjects for which she or he has an insufficient knowledge base, when an instructor misinterprets research evidence to support a theory or social policy favored by the instructor, or when an instructor responsible for a prerequisite survey course teaches only those topics in which the instructor has a personal interest.

PRINCIPLE 2: Pedagogical Competence
> A pedagogically competent teacher communicates the objectives of the course
> to students, is aware of alternative instructional methods or strategies, and selects
> methods of instruction that, according to research evidence (including personal
> or self-reflective research), are effective in helping students to achieve the course
> objectives.

This principle implies that, in addition to knowing the subject matter, a teacher has adequate pedagogical knowledge and skills, including communication of objectives, selection of effective instructional methods, providing opportunity for practice and feedback, and dealing with student diversity. If mastery of a certain skill (for example, critical analysis or design of experiments) is part of the course objectives and will be considered in evaluation and grading of students, the teacher provides students with adequate opportunity to practice and receive feedback on that skill during the course. If learning styles differ significantly for different students or groups of students, the teacher is aware of these differences and, if feasible, varies her or his style of teaching accordingly.

To maintain pedagogical competence, an instructor takes active steps to stay current regarding teaching strategies that will help students learn relevant knowledge and skills and will provide equal educational opportunity for diverse groups. This might involve reading general or discipline-specific educational literature, attending workshops and conferences, or experimentation with alternative methods of teaching a given course or a specific group of students. A specific example of failure to fulfill the principle of pedagogical competence would be to use an instructional method or assessment method that is incongruent with the stated course objectives (for example, using exams consisting solely of fact-memorization questions when the main objective of the course is to teach problem-solving skills). Another example would be to fail to give students adequate opportunity to practice or learn skills that are included in the course objectives and will be tested on the final exam.

PRINCIPLE 3: Dealing with Sensitive Topics
> Topics that students are likely to find sensitive or discomforting are dealt with in an open, honest, and positive way.

Among other things, this principle means that the teacher acknowledges from the outset that a particular topic is sensitive, and explains why it is necessary to include it in the course syllabus. Also, the teacher identifies his or her own perspective on the issue and compares it to alternative approaches or interpretations, thereby providing students with an understanding of the complexity of the issue and the difficulty of achieving a single "objective" conclusion. Finally, in order to provide a safe and open environment for class discussion, the teacher invites all students to state their positions on the issue, sets ground rules for discussion, is respectful of students even when it is necessary to disagree, and encourages students to be respectful of one another.

As one example of a sensitive topic, analysis of certain poems written by John Donne can cause distress among students who perceive racial slurs embedded in the professor's interpretation, particularly if that interpretation is presented as the authoritative reading of the poem. As a result, some students may view the class as closed and exclusive rather than open and inclusive. A reasonable option is for the professor's analysis of the poem to be followed by an open class discussion of other possible interpretations and the pros and cons of each.

Another example of a sensitive topic occurs when a film depicting scenes of child abuse is shown, without forewarning, in a developmental psychology class. Assuming that such a film has a valid pedagogical role, student distress and discomfort can be minimized by warning students in advance of the content of the film, explaining why it is included in the curriculum, and providing opportunities for students to discuss their reactions to the film.

PRINCIPLE 4: Student Development
> The overriding responsibility of the teacher is to contribute to the intellectual development of the student, at least in the context of the teacher's own area of

expertise, and to avoid actions such as exploitation and discrimination that detract from student development.

According to this principle, the teacher's most basic responsibilities are to design instruction that facilitates learning and encourages autonomy and independent thinking in students, to treat students with respect and dignity, and to avoid actions that detract unjustifiably from student development. Failure to take responsibility for student development occurs when a teacher comes to class underprepared, fails to design effective instruction, coerces students to adopt a particular value or point of view, or fails to discuss alternative theoretical interpretations (see also Principles 1, 2, and 3).

Less obvious examples of failure to take responsibility for student development occur when teachers ignore the power differential between themselves and students and behave in ways that exploit or denigrate students. Such behaviors include sexual or racial discrimination; derogatory comments toward students; taking primary or sole authorship of a publication reporting research conceptualized, designed, and conducted by a student collaborator; failure to acknowledge academic or intellectual debts to students; and assigning research work to students that serves the ends of the teacher but is unrelated to the educational goals of the course.

In some cases, the teacher's responsibility to contribute to student development can come into conflict with responsibilities to other agencies, such as the university, the academic discipline, or society as a whole. This can happen, for example, when a marginal student requests a letter of reference in support of advanced education, or when a student with learning disabilities requests accommodations that require modification of normal grading standards or graduation requirements. There are no hard and fast rules that govern situations such as these. The teacher must weigh all conflicting responsibilities, possibly consult with other individuals, and come to a reasoned decision.

PRINCIPLE 5: Dual Relationships with Students

> To avoid conflict of interest, a teacher does not enter into dual-role relationships with students that are likely to detract from student development or lead to actual or perceived favoritism on the part of the teacher.

This principle means that it is the responsibility of the teacher to keep relationships with students focused on pedagogical goals and academic requirements. The most obvious example of a dual relationship that is likely to impair teacher objectivity and/or detract from student development is any form of sexual or close personal relationship with a current student. Other potentially problematic dual relationships include accepting a teaching (or grading) role with respect to a member of one's immediate family, a close friend, or an individual who is also a client, patient, or business partner; excessive socializing with students outside of class, either individually or as a group; lending money to or borrowing money from students; giving gifts to or accepting gifts from students; and introducing a course requirement that students participate in a political movement advocated by the instructor.

Even if the teacher believes that she or he is maintaining objectivity in situations such as these, the perception of favoritism on the part of other students is as educationally disastrous as actual favoritism or unfairness. If a teacher becomes involved in a dual relationship with a student, despite efforts to the contrary, it is the responsibility of the teacher to notify his or her supervisor of the situation as soon as possible, so that alternative arrangements can be made for supervision or evaluation of the student.

Although there are definite pedagogical benefits to establishing good rapport with students and interacting with students both inside and outside the classroom, there are also serious risks of exploitation, compromise of academic standards, and harm to student development. It is the responsibility of the teacher to prevent these risks from materializing into real or perceived conflicts of interest.

Principle 6: Confidentiality

Student grades, attendance records, and private communications are treated as confidential materials and are released only with student consent, for legitimate academic purposes, or if there are reasonable grounds for believing that releasing such information will be beneficial to the student or will prevent harm to others.

This principle suggests that students are entitled to the same level of confidentiality in their relationships with teachers as would exist in a lawyer-client or doctor-patient relationship. Violation of confidentiality in the teacher-student relationship can cause students to distrust teachers and to show decreased academic motivation. Whatever rules or policies are followed with respect to confidentiality of student records should be disclosed in full to students at the beginning of the academic term.

It could be argued that in the absence of adequate grounds (that is, student consent, legitimate purpose, or benefit to the student) any of the following could be construed as a violation of confidentiality: providing academic records to a potential employer, researcher, or private investigator; discussing a student's grades or academic problems with another faculty member; and using privately communicated student experiences as teaching or research materials. Similarly, leaving graded student papers or exams in a pile outside one's office makes it possible for any student to determine any other student's grade and thus fails to protect the confidentiality of individual student grades. This problem can be avoided by having students pick up their papers individually during office hours, or by returning papers with no grade or identifying information visible on the cover page.

Principle 7: Respect for Colleagues

A university teacher respects the dignity of her or his colleagues and works cooperatively with colleagues in the interest of fostering student development.

This principle means that in interactions among colleagues with respect to teaching, the overriding concern is the development of students. Disagreements between colleagues relating to teaching are settled privately, if possible, with no harm to student development. If a teacher suspects that a colleague has shown incompetence or ethical violations in teaching, the teacher takes responsibility for investigating the matter thoroughly and consulting privately with the colleague before taking further action.

A specific example of failure to show respect for colleagues occurs when a teacher makes unwarranted derogatory comments in the classroom about the competence of another teacher. For example, Professor A tells students that information provided to them last year by Professor B is of no use and will be replaced by information from Professor A in the course at hand. Other examples of failure to uphold this principle would be a curriculum committee's refusing to require courses in other departments that compete with their own department for student enrolment; or Professor X's refusing a student permission to take a course from Professor Y, who is disliked by Professor X, even though the course would be useful to the student.

PRINCIPLE 8: Valid Assessment of Students

> Given the importance of assessment of student performance in university teaching and in students' lives and careers, instructors are responsible for taking adequate steps to ensure that assessment of students is valid, open, fair, and congruent with course objectives.

This principle means that the teacher is aware of research (including personal or self-reflective research) on the advantages and disadvantages of alternative methods of assessment, and based on this knowledge the teacher selects assessment techniques that are consistent with the objectives of the course and at the same time are as reliable and valid as possible. Furthermore, assessment procedures and grading standards are communicated clearly to students at the beginning of the course, and except in rare circumstances there is no deviation from the announced procedures. Student exams, papers, and assignments are graded carefully and fairly through the use of a rational marking system that can be communicated to students. By means appropriate to the size of the class, students are provided with prompt and accurate feedback on their performance at regular intervals throughout the course, an explanation of how their work was graded, and constructive suggestions for improving their standing in the course. In a similar vein, teachers are fair and objective in writing letters of reference for students.

One example of an ethically questionable assessment practice is to grade students on skills that were not part of the announced course objectives and/or were not allocated adequate practice opportunity during the course. If students are expected to demonstrate critical inquiry skills on the final exam, they should have been given the opportunity to develop critical inquiry skills during the course. Another violation of valid assessment occurs when faculty members teaching two different sections of the same course use drastically different assessment procedures or grading standards, so that the same level of student performance earns significantly different final grades in the two sections.

PRINCIPLE 9: Respect for Institution

> In the interests of student development, a university teacher is aware of and respects the educational goals, policies, and standards of the institution in which he or she teaches.

This principle implies that a teacher shares a collective responsibility to work for the good of the university as a whole, to uphold the educational goals and standards of the university, and to abide by university policies and regulations pertaining to the education of students.

Specific examples of failure to uphold the principle of respect for institution include engaging in excessive work activity outside the university that conflicts with university teaching responsibilities and being unaware of or ignoring valid university regulations on provision of course outlines, scheduling of exams, or academic misconduct.

Conclusions

This document was written by individuals actively involved in university teaching, each of whom has strong views on the importance of teaching and the responsibilities of university professors with respect to teaching. The authors believe that implementation of an ethical code similar to that described herein would contribute to the overall improvement of teaching in colleges and universities.

References

The authors are indebted to the following sources for ideas that were incorporated into the STLHE document:

American Psychological Association. "Ethical Principles of Psychologists." *American Psychologist*, 1990, *45*, 390–395.

Code of Professional Ethics for Academic Staff. Calgary, Alta.: University of Calgary, 1994.

Matthews, J. R. "The Teaching of Ethics and the Ethics of Teaching." *Teaching of Psychology*, 1991, *18*, 80–85.

HARRY MURRAY, EILEEN GILLESE, MADELINE LENNON, PAUL MERCER, and MARILYN ROBINSON are faculty members in the disciplines of psychology, law, visual arts, physiology, and physiology/educational development, respectively, at the University of Western Ontario. All five authors are members of the Society for Teaching and Learning in Higher Education, and all five are recipients of the 3M Canada award for excellence in university teaching.

Sound ethical decisions depend on clear problem definition, careful review of alternatives, consideration of consequences, and thoughtful application of relevant principles of responsibility. Often they also require our willingness to receive corrective insight and to check our judgments with our moral intuitions.

Making Responsible Academic Ethical Decisions

Charles H. Reynolds

Ethics, when critical and based on good reasons for action, is not merely subjective discourse. H. Richard Niebuhr (1960, 1963, 1989) and John Rawls (1971, 1993) have each made distinctive contributions to an understanding of responsible moral judgment. I will review aspects of their work in this chapter in part to indicate how it is possible for moral judgment to be based on good public reasons within an ethics of responsibility, but also to sketch other distinctive features of this approach to ethics. Despite what many may think, a rational debate about ethical decisions and ethical theory is possible. Niebuhr and Rawls provide ways for one to present public reasons for both agreements and disagreements in ethical judgments.

A limited range of personal, professional, systemic, public, and political principles of academic responsibility are reprinted below. These principles are not stated in lexical order—in other words, certain principles do not always take precedence over other stated principles, as is the case in Rawls's principles of justice. But importantly, these academic principles secure a respect for the intrinsic value of persons and the unqualified quest for truth, deep values essential for a community of inquiry and learning. This account of the deep values of respect for persons and commitment to truth, and of principles that secure these values, represents an objective and public account of the academic virtues. These virtues distinguish colleges and universities as social institutions.

Higher education has a special responsibility to itself, to its students, to the learned professions, and to the society that provides the economic resources to make our colleges and universities possible. That responsibility is to examine—with care—ways to cultivate responsible judgment. Colleges and

Academic Principles of Responsibility

Personal Principles

Everyone in an academic community has responsibilities to
   1.1 demonstrate a respect for each person as an individual
   1.2 communicate honestly and truthfully with all persons
   1.3 enhance the self-esteem of other persons
   1.4 help build fair and compassionate social and cultural systems that promote the common good of all persons

Professional Principles

Professionals associated with a college or university have responsibilities to
   2.1 assist their institution to fulfill its educational mission
   2.2 strive to enhance the personal and intellectual development of other persons
   2.3 be compassionate, thorough, and fair in assessing the performance of students and professional associates
   2.4 exercise the authority of their office in ways that respect persons and avoid the abuse of power
   2.5 conduct their professional activities in ways that uphold or surpass the ideals of virtue and competence

Systemic Principles

Colleges and universities have systemic responsibilities to
   3.1 be fair, keep agreements and promises, operate within the framework of the law, and extend due process to all persons
   3.2 strive for an efficient and effective management that enables the institution to adapt to new opportunities
   3.3 be compassionate and humane in all relationships while protecting the safety of persons and property
   3.4 articulate their missions in ways that reflect their actual strengths and aspirations
   3.5 foster policies that build a community of racial and socioeconomic diversity
   3.6 assist members in their professional development while requiring competent performance from everyone
   3.7 support an internal policy that fosters and protects academic freedom

Public Principles

Colleges and universities have public responsibilities to
   4.1 serve as examples in our public life of open institutions where truthful communications are required
   4.2 preserve human wisdom while conducting research to create new forms of knowledge
   4.3 serve the public interest in ways compatible with being an academic institution
   4.4 enhance the development of international understanding and support the world community of scholars
   4.5 promote a critical appreciation of the creative activity of the human imagination
   4.6 interpret academic values to their constituencies

Political Principles

Colleges and universities have political responsibilities to
5.1 promote forms of policy based on an equal respect for persons
5.2 foster policies that increase access to higher education for the poor, minorities, and other underserved populations
5.3 help develop fair and compassionate means of resolving conflict between persons, groups, and nations
5.4 nurture a community of responsibility that is sensitive to the needs of future generations
5.5 be good corporate citizens in all external relations

Reynolds and Smith, 1990.

universities can take the risk of giving moral leadership to the modern world. We do ourselves, our students, and our society a disservice whenever we leave the impression that education is merely to establish technical competence in a specialized area of knowledge.

Education is not, and has never been, a value-neutral activity. To be sure, at times educators have self-consciously acknowledged and fostered their ethical responsibilities, and at other times somewhat neglected them. Moreover, at times moral zealots have tried to appeal to ethics to limit free inquiry or to provide a moral reason for restricting the open quest for public knowledge. The academy has rightly resisted these efforts to redefine the academic virtues, which almost any restrictions on free inquiry or on the free exchange of information necessarily entail. I hold that free inquiry and the free exchange of information can only be limited if such restrictions are required to secure open institutions where free inquiry flourishes. All resistance by the academy to restrictions on free inquiry powerfully demonstrates the commitment of the academy to its most basic professional virtues. Cynics wrongly infer that the academy is ethically neutral when it challenges all alien conceptions of morality.

Academicians are frequently confronted with three important types of assessment: they must assess persons—indeed, both the skills and character of persons; they must assess institutional policies, priorities, and procedures; and they must assess the quality, effectiveness, and productivity of institutional programs. Although these three types of assessment are distinguishable, they share similar characteristics. The skill to make discerning judgments in each of these three areas helps to form a community of responsibility, provided public reasons are offered to support these assessment decisions. For this skill to flourish, an ethics of responsibility is required.

The academic principles can inform both personal and institutional actions, and build a community of responsibility, if they are supported by an ethics of responsibility and a rational decision procedure for making moral decisions. Niebuhr (1963) gave a more precise formulation to Max Weber's notion of an ethics of responsibility (Gerth and Mills, 1946). A responsible agent, according to Niebuhr, develops the skill to discern a fitting response in a situation requiring moral choice. In the remainder of this chapter, I will review Niebuhr's contributions to formulating an ethics of responsibility, contrast Niebuhr's work with aspects of the theory of ethics proposed by John Rawls, and conclude by proposing a decision procedure for making moral decisions that fully utilizes the principles of responsibility.

Niebuhr's Moments of Discerning Judgment

Niebuhr's isolation of four moments of discerning judgment in his ethics of responsibility can be an important asset for educators. The fitting action by a responsible agent includes, but is not reducible to Weber's emphasis on taking account of the consequences of actions. Niebuhr (1963, p. 65) characterized his notion of an ethics of responsibility. "The idea or pattern of responsibility, then, may summarily and abstractly be defined as the idea of an agent's action as response to an action upon him in accordance with his interpretation of the latter action and with his expectation of response to his response; and all of this is in a continuing community of agents." In developing his ethics of responsibility, Niebuhr focuses on the qualities of discerning judgment that enable an agent to respond to a situation in a fitting way. Niebuhr characterizes four distinct moments of discerning judgment.

The first of these moments is the *response* an agent makes in a situation to external factors that require action. What is going on? To what is one being summoned to respond? Niebuhr's existential insight here is that one does not volunteer for ethical dilemmas; rather, one finds oneself confronted with external forces that impinge upon one and require a response.

If you recall difficult ethical issues you have confronted, I think you will agree that the element of response to external factors acting upon you represents a critical moment for discerning judgment. It is essential that one develop the capacity to react to actual external factors instead of reacting in routine ways that fail to distinguish a new situation from a similar, but different, previous situation. A disposition to respond to novel external factors without becoming closed or defensive is a critical first moment in discerning judgment. An insecurity that makes it difficult for one to acknowledge the reality of one's actual environment, a lazy or unquestioning mind that does not explore one's actual world, and an ignorant or uninformed mind that cannot comprehend the reality of the actual world can each contribute to failure in this moment of discerning judgment.

The act of *interpretation* is the second moment in discerning judgment. The responsible agent first identifies and then interprets the significance of the external factors acting upon him or her. For Niebuhr, this moment requires an imaginative ability to discern the fitting response to a particular situation while being aware of the complete context of the decision. Here it is necessary to supplement Niebuhr's important work on moral discernment with the principles of responsibility.

The principles of responsibility identify relevant and salient factors that one should consider in making an ethical decision. But the principles can at best provide guidance for a discerning judge, and an element of risk and creativity is always involved in interpreting a situation with the aid of the principles. Furthermore, it is possible for reasonable people to disagree over which principles apply in which situations. But the principles can assist those who disagree to explain to one another the reasons for their disagreements. Ideological rigidity, on the one hand, and an absence of commitments, on the other, are the most likely causes of mistakes in this moment of judgment.

The third moment in discerning judgment is an agent's *imaginative anticipation* of responses to his or her decision. For Niebuhr, this moment includes the importance of taking account of the consequences of an action; but unlike those utilitarians who think all moral actions aim at producing the greatest amount of good, Niebuhr does not hold that the morality of an action depends exclusively on maximizing certain goals or outcomes. The being of the agent—his or her character—is valued by Niebuhr in ways that do not depend exclusively on the consequences of the agent's actions. Moreover, the principles of responsibility—as independent right-making characteristics of a discerning judgment—make a claim on an agent in ways that do not depend exclusively on their contribution to some notion of a greatest good. Both an adherence to rules without regard to their social consequences and a focus on social consequences without respect for rules or principles can distort this moment of judgment.

The fourth moment in discerning judgment is an agent's taking account of the reality that he or she *participates in a community of solidarity* with all other beings and has a relationship and responsibility to the Whole. Responsible agents identify with and belong to the world they react to, interpret, and creatively shape. They are loyal to the community of responsibility they share with all other moral agents and affirm their destiny in relation to their total environment and to the cosmos. A reductionistic naturalism that fails to appreciate the distinctive grandeur of the human proprium, or a pompous humanism that fails to affirm continuities and mutual dependencies among all beings, can each distort this moment of responsible judgment.

The four moments are intrinsic aspects of discerning judgment. In this model of judgment, an agent imaginatively and sympathetically reviews a situation, examines all features of that situation as fully and impartially as possible, and weighs with care and deliberation the principles of responsibility that fit that situation. The agent then risks a moral judgment and action that he or she will stand behind until reasons are provided for why the action should be revised in this or that way to be more fitting, everything considered. Because human agents are never fully informed, completely impartial, capable of imagining all potential consequences of an action, or capable of having empathy for all being, Niebuhr advocates a stance of resolved humility—a *willingness to receive corrective insight* from other similarly situated agents—as in solidarity we strive to improve our individual and institutional capacities to make responsible public judgments. The ideal is a cooperative quest and an unfinished skill for human agents.

Rawls's Principles of Justice

In his classic work on justice, Rawls (1971) uses the traditional metaphor of the social contract to examine the comparative rationality of justice as fairness over rival theories of justice. Rawls argues that under conditions of fair choice two principles of justice—a *liberty* principle and an *equality* principle, placed in lexical order—would be selected by rational parties to secure their mutual self-interests if the subject of justice is understood to be the basic structure of society.

Rawls's use of the social contract metaphor with the gradually lifting veil addresses at the methodological level potential sources of disagreement for the contracting parties as they choose the normative principles and rules to regulate the basic structure of their society. The veil is combined with the other features of the "original situation" to ensure that the parties choosing among conceptions of justice will share the impartiality constraints of the moral point of view, will have a similar motivational system, and will all share the general information about society that makes a conception of justice both necessary and possible to regulate institutional and individual actions.

Rawls's metaphorical situation of choice is designed to rule out the sources of disagreement that distort discerning judgment. The result is that one person's rational choice will necessarily be a rational choice for any other person. Rawls provides a conception of a public ethic. The assumptions of his argument are stated with sufficient clarity to enable any rational person to agree or disagree with him as he develops his theory. For this reason, the details of Rawls's argument are less important than the formal structure he uses that makes a rational, public argument about ethics possible.

Under the actual conditions in which academic decisions are made, no statement of principles will provide the unambiguous moral guidance that some would prefer to have. At times principles are more useful for explaining disagreements than for forging agreements. Moreover, when supplemented by Niebuhr's ethic of responsibility and a decision procedure for making moral decisions, the principles can serve as helpful guides for making rational and public decisions.

There is one aspect of Rawls's theory that is critical for how one can best appropriate and use the principles of responsibility. I refer to his notion of reflective equilibrium. For Rawls, *any ethical judgment may be checked by our moral intuitions when we contemplate that matter as conscientiously as possible.* He believes there should normally be a fit between our considered moral sense and our best ethical judgment about that same matter. Rawls recognizes that at times this fit will not be present and that we will need to revise either our considered moral sense or our best theoretical judgment. This is Rawls's way of respecting both our individual experience and the communal traditions that have shaped our moral sensibilities. I appropriate this same check below, using the example of a professor's final course grades.

Steps in Making a Moral Decision

1. *Define the concrete ethical issues.* A student approached a department chair with a complaint about the scheduling of his final examination. Rather than give the final examination on the day and time scheduled, his professor scheduled a number of oral examinations for individual students at times throughout the examination week. The oral examination for this student was scheduled on a day when he had made plans to be out of state to accompany his mother to a criminal trial. He requested the faculty member to change the day of his oral examination from Tuesday to Wednesday. The faculty member refused and said the student did not have sufficient reason to change the date of the examination. The student then appealed to the department chair.

The department chair called the student's mother to verify that she needed her son to appear in court with her. The mother was very clear about the need for her son to accompany her to court. The department chair then advised the faculty member to give the student his oral examination on Wednesday as the student had requested. The faculty member agreed to this change and gave the student his oral examination on the following Wednesday. After the examination was completed, the faculty member informed the student that he had failed the examination and the course for procedural reasons. The faculty member said that he could be ordered by the chair of his department to change the time of a student's examination, but that it was within his academic freedom to assign the student a grade. The student was very angry and upset as he related the faculty member's action to the department chair. He thought the faculty member was abusing his power of office (Academic Principle of Responsibility 2.4) and was being unfair in his method of assessing the student's performance (A.P.R. 2.3).

2. *Imaginatively review the alternatives for resolving the issue.* The department chair first met with the faculty member to determine if the facts reported by the student were true. The faculty member verified the student's report and said that his academic freedom would be violated unless his assignment of a failing grade to the student were allowed to stand.

The first alternative considered by the department chair was that he would appoint one person to a review committee, the aggrieved faculty member would appoint a second person, and the two appointees would select a third. This three-person committee would review the student's complaint and the faculty member's actions and make a recommendation back to the department chair. The faculty member rejected this proposal also in the name of academic freedom. He said that no faculty committee had the right to review the grade he had assigned the student.

The university had no official policy on how students could appeal faculty-assigned grades. The informal policy was that some department chairs would change a grade they thought was inappropriate and other chairs would consult with a faculty member about a grade but would leave the final decision on the grade to the faculty member. The department chair in this case did not believe the assigned failure could be permitted to stand. He consulted with the tenured faculty in his department and they were unable to reach a consensus on what action should be taken.

The department chair approached the faculty member in this case and requested all information relevant for evaluating the student in question and informed the faculty member that the student should be given the grade earned in the class. Rather than turn over the requested information, the faculty member destroyed all grades and evaluation information for all the students he was teaching that term. He then turned in an "A" for all students except for the student who brought the complaint. He turned in an "F" for that student. The faculty member then submitted a letter of resignation in which he accused the department chair of infringing on his academic freedom. What should this department chair now do?

3. *Carefully consider each alternative in relation to its future consequences and its possible relation to the principles of responsibility.* Because the department chair agreed with the student that the faculty member had abused the power of his office (A.P.R. 2.4) and had not been fair in his assessment of students (A.P.R. 2.3), the department chair recommended to the chief academic officer that the resignation be accepted. It was.

With all academic records destroyed, there was no way to establish the proper grades for the almost one hundred students who received an "A", nor for establishing the proper grade for the student who received an "F". The department chair was unwilling to give a grade with no basis for assigning one. The chair changed the failure to an incomplete and permitted the student to retake the class the next term. The student in the case was in the process of applying to law schools. The department chair wrote a letter to the relevant law schools explaining the reasons for the incomplete in the class and why it should therefore be ignored. The student retook the class with a different faculty member and made an "A". That grade was immediately sent to the relevant law schools. The student had several acceptances and has now graduated from law school.

4. *Imaginatively review your preferred resolution of the issue by checking the proposed solution with your intuitive moral judgment.* View the issue with sympathy for all affected parties, take full account of all the relevant facts, be as impartial in your judgment as you can be, and ask yourself which alternative strikes you as morally preferable. If possible, imagine yourself as the persons (in the different relevant roles) who are likely to be most affected by the decision made. If your intuitive moral judgment fits your judgment as guided by the principles of responsibility, you have likely made an informed moral judgment. If your intuitive judgment does not match your judgment as guided by the principles of responsibility (and other relevant value considerations, since no listing of principles can represent all relevant values), go back and review steps two and three.

In this case, the department chair reported that his intuitive moral judgment and the academic principles of responsibility led him to the same decision. He did, however, report that the statement of the principles aided his reflection. Following this case, the university in question adopted a written set of policies and guidelines for student grade appeals. New policies were also adopted concerning how a faculty member could deviate from giving final examinations at the date and time assigned by the registrar. This particular case was resolved.

If you are trying to resolve a case and you have a problem with a fit between your intuitive judgment and your judgment as guided by the principles (and other relevant value considerations), first reconsider step one. It may be that you are dealing with a policy issue rather than a moral issue that the principles of responsibility can provide help in resolving. You may be dealing primarily with a legal issue (in which case you may be aware of your need for legal counsel) or with an institutional value issue that can better be guided by an institutional story than by an abstract principle.

If you continue to believe you are dealing with an ethical issue in which the principles should be helpful, but you are still unable to reach a decision, then again rethink the principles of responsibility as they relate to your issue. You may need to revise one of the principles to attain a fit with your considered moral judgment, or you may need to revise your considered judgment. This is the important insight from Rawls mentioned above. If you need to revise a statement of a principle of responsibility and if your revision is based on the deep values of respect for persons and commitment to truthful communication, then it is likely to be a revision that will be compatible with the other principles.

5. *Act on your best deliberative judgment.* The principles, guided by the moral imagination that makes discerning judgment possible and supplemented by other action guides, can be used to assist a responsible person to make an informed judgment about a complicated ethical dilemma that he or she can then communicate with confidence to others.

This decision procedure should help a person critically engage anyone who would decide an ethical issue in an apparently different way. It is frequently more important to understand the reasons for an ethical disagreement than it is to understand why and how an agreement has been reached.

References

Gerth, H. H., and Mills, C. W. *From Max Weber: Essays in Sociology.* New York: Oxford University Press, 1946.

Niebuhr, H. R. *Radical Monotheism and Western Culture.* New York: Harper and Brothers, 1960.

Niebuhr, H. R. *The Responsible Self: An Essay in Christian Moral Philosophy.* New York: Harper & Row, 1963.

Niebuhr, H. R. *Faith on Earth: An Inquiry into the Structure of Human Faith.* New Haven, Conn.: Yale University Press, 1989.

Rawls, J. *A Theory of Justice.* Cambridge Mass.: Harvard University Press, 1971.
Rawls, J. *Political Liberalism.* New York: Columbia University Press, 1993.
Reynolds, C., and Smith, D. "Academic Principles of Responsibility." In W. W. May (ed.), *Ethics and Higher Education.* New York: American Council on Education, 1990.

CHARLES H. REYNOLDS *is professor and head of religious studies at the University of Tennessee, Knoxville.*

Confronting a colleague who is suspected of unethical conduct is never easy or pleasant. Observing appropriate procedures may help facilitate a successful outcome.

Intervening with Colleagues

Patricia Keith-Spiegel, Arno F. Wittig, David V. Perkins, Deborah Ware Balogh, Bernard E. Whitley, Jr.

A direct observer of an ethically problematic act is often the most logical person to attempt to mitigate it. Indeed, many of the grayer instances may require collegial intervention lest the questionable practice or action persist. Authors of professor-bashing books often accuse college and university faculties of protecting each other, ignoring blatantly unethical actions, and supporting a conspiracy of mediocrity and fraud. Although one may refute these overgeneralized and often overblown charges, it is far better and ultimately more productive to take a strong, proactive role in facilitating internally generated solutions to the greatest extent possible.

It is easy enough for us to strongly encourage direct and active involvement in a situation involving ethically questionable behavior of colleagues. However, actually getting involved is quite another matter. These are people one faces every day, people one may live with for thirty more years. Some are friends. Some are disliked. Some hold higher rank and, therefore, power that could be wielded in revenge. Even in academia, a person who attempts to intervene when he or she perceives an ethical problem may be viewed as arrogant and self-righteous, or even as a troublemaker and a "snitch." The decision to intervene and the method of confrontation will depend, to some extent, on the nature of the extant relationship and any power differentials. We offer some suggestions, adapted from Keith-Spiegel and Koocher (1985), for approaching colleagues who may be exhibiting unethical behavior.

This material is reprinted, with permission, from *Ethics in Teaching: A Casebook,* by Patricia Keith-Spiegel, Arno F. Wittig, David V. Perkins, Deborah Ware Balogh, and Bernard E. Whitley, Jr. Muncie, Ind.: Ball State University, 1993.

1. Objectively determine what ethical principle, policy, or moral code of conduct has been violated. Consider why it is wrong, what harms may have accrued or could accrue, and how the integrity or image of the department, school, or institution may have been (or could be) compromised. Ask what legitimate loyalties may be in conflict. This preconfrontation exercise will assist in clarifying your duty and raising your self-confidence and commitment.

2. Attempt to assess the strength of your evidence that a violation has been committed. Is it mostly hearsay? How credible is the source of information? This procedure is important because it assists in making a decision to intervene at this point and helps with formulating the appropriate approach for confrontation, as will be discussed more fully.

3. Be aware of your own motivations to engage in (or to avoid) a confrontation. In addition to any fears, angers, or other affective reactions, do you perceive that the conduct as it stands, or if it continues, could harm the integrity of the teaching profession or harm one or more of the people involved? If the answer to this question is affirmative, then some form of action is required.

4. Consultation with a trusted and experienced colleague who has demonstrated a sensitivity to ethical issues is recommended at this point. If you personally do not know such a person, professional organizations may provide assistance or recommend a colleague in the field who can be consulted.

5. Schedule a confrontation in advance, but not in a menacing way. (For example, do *not* say, "Something has come to my attention about you that causes me grave concern and that I must talk to you about. What are you doing a week from Thursday?") Rather, indicate to the suspected offender that you would like to speak privately, and schedule a face-to-face meeting. An office setting would normally be more appropriate than a home or restaurant. Handling such matters over the phone is not recommended.

6. When entering into a confrontation phase, remain calm and self-confident. The suspected offender may display considerable emotion. Expect that, but do not fall into it. Remain nonthreatening. Avoid a rigidly moralistic, holier-than-thou demeanor; most people find that approach obnoxious.

7. Set the tone for a constructive and educative session. Your role is *not* that of accuser, judge, jury, or penance-dispenser. Instead, perceive your role as one of informing and educating, as a teammate in problem solving. The session will probably develop better if you see yourself as creating an alliance with the person, not in the sense of consensus and loyalty, but as colleagues facing a problem together. You might use such phrases as, "I am confused about why you choose to do it this way" or "Something came to my attention that perplexed me, and I thought maybe we could discuss it." This approach can be less threatening than a direct accusation and may elicit your colleague's rationale rather than just defensiveness.

8. If confidences require protection (another person agrees to allow you to confront the colleague, for example, but insists that his or her identity be

protected), explain this circumstance and expect an uncomfortable reaction. No one relishes an unseen and unknown accuser. You should also advise the informant that it is unlikely any formal action would be taken unless he or she agrees to be identified.

9. Allow the suspected offender time to explain and defend in as much detail as is required. The colleague may be flustered and repetitive. Be patient.

10. If the colleague becomes abusive or threatening, attempt to head toward a more constructive state. Although some people need a chance to vent feelings, they often settle down if the confronting person remains steady and refrains from becoming abusive and threatening in return. If a negative reaction continues, it might be appropriate to say something calming such as "I see you are very upset right now and I regret that we cannot explore this matter together in a way that would be satisfactory for both of us. If you would like to think about what I have presented to you, and if you would reconsider talking about it, please call me within a week." If a return call is not forthcoming, then other forms of action should be considered.

11. If the suspected offender is a friend or acquaintance with whom there have been no previous problematic interactions, the "teammate role" described above is easier to implement. You can suggest that you want to be the one to deal with the matter because you care about the person and his or her professional standing. The danger, of course, is that you may feel that you are risking an established, positive relationship. If this effort works, however, you have done your friend a favor through protection from embarrassment or from more public forms of censure. Discomfort, to the extent that it ensues, will probably be temporary.

12. If the suspected offender is someone you dislike, the disposition will be, by definition, more difficult. If the information is known to others or can be shared appropriately with others, you might consider asking someone who has a better relationship with this person to intercede. If that course is not possible, and if objective introspection reveals the conclusion that the misconduct requires intervention on its own merits regardless of who committed it, then some form of action is necessary.

13. If the suspected offender is of higher rank or holds a position of power over you, you may be able to get the support of someone not affected by the person's position. We encourage the establishment of a mentor system in every department so that junior faculty members have a senior colleague with whom they can speak freely about such issues as these.

Confronting a colleague about an ethical concern is in the same league as calling in a student suspected of cheating. However, courage to help maintain the integrity of the profession is worth a summons. We discourage the exercise of the two safer-feeling but less effective alternatives: gossip and sending anonymous notes. Neither can guarantee a solution to the problem, and both have a high potential for making things worse. Finally, we do recognize that not all ethical dilemmas are amenable to informal resolution. Sometimes one will have no choice but to report a problem to one's supervisor or other institutional office. If entire departments become embroiled in matters with ethical ramifications, formal intervention, perhaps involving a skilled mediator, is indicated.

Reference

Keith-Spiegel, P., and G. P. Koocher. *Ethics in Psychology: Professional Standards and Cases.* New York: McGraw-Hill, 1985.

PATRICIA KEITH-SPIEGEL, ARNO F. WITTIG, DAVID V. PERKINS, DEBORAH WARE BALOGH, and BERNARD E. WHITLEY, JR., are faculty members in the department of psychological science at Ball State University.

Our actions, however well intended, may lead to unethical behavior, unexpected consequences, and even the very results that we try to avoid. Through critical reflection we can discover ways to avert these outcomes.

Reflecting on the Ethics and Values of Our Practice

Ronald A. Smith

Consider the following two professors. Each is very concerned about the quality of a student's work and wants to be helpful.

> Professor C is very disturbed by the recent deterioration in the work submitted by one of his students. He wants to help her but is not sure how he should approach her. He has noticed that she seems to be under quite a bit of strain lately, and he thinks of her as somewhat "fragile." He wants to encourage her, but he is worried about saying something that might add to her upset. Thus, he decides to ease in to the topic of her work by asking questions such as "How is school going?" and "How do you think you are doing in the course?"

> Professor J is upset by a recent "attitude" problem on the part of one of her students. She feels this has led to a deterioration in his work. She has spoken to him before, but nothing much seems to have changed. She decides that she has to be fairly honest with him. Thus, she begins her conversation bluntly with "Your performance is really not up to the standard for this course. I feel as though you have a chip on your shoulder. If there is not a marked improvement in your work, I think you will fail the course. I'd like to talk about your future in the course and the program."

In each case, the professor chooses an action strategy—to ease in (Professor C), to be bluntly honest (Professor J)—in order to be helpful to the student. These strategies, which flow from good intentions, may have unintended consequences and paradoxically may even produce the very results they were designed to avoid.

Professor C's easing in, which is designed to avoid upsetting his student, may be interpreted by her as an indication that her work is so bad and she is so weak that she can't handle the truth. She may also assume his indirectness is a sign that these issues can't be discussed openly. These interpretations could easily cause her to become upset. They might also cause her to withhold her feelings because these issues to her may not seem discussable with Professor C.

Professor J's student may interpret J's blunt honesty as a clear indication that she has made up her mind and is not interested in any discussion of his point of view. Thus, he might conclude she is not really interested in talking with him about his future, but only in telling him what she has already decided. His reactions, based on his interpretations of her behavior, could easily be seen as reflecting an "attitude." It is unlikely that any of this will be discussed in a helpful manner if he believes that Professor J is closed to gaining more information and insight.

In this chapter, I present a framework within which to examine how teaching professionals such as Professors C and J think and act in difficult situations in their practice. I focus on some critical questions: what rules do we follow when we make decisions about how to act in difficult situations with our students? What does it mean to be caring, honest, just, helpful, or encouraging? To what extent are our actions consistent with the values we proclaim? Do they produce the results we intend? To what extent are we aware of the gaps between what we intend and what we actually produce? More importantly, do we behave in ways that increase the likelihood that we will learn about the impact of our actions and learn how to be more effective in the future?

In particular, I focus on the *ethics* of our practice, those *rules that inform our actions*. I focus not only on the "shoulds" and "oughts" that we espouse, but also on our action strategies and governing values that can be inferred from a careful examination of what we actually do. The ultimate purpose of this critical reflection on our practice is to discover ways to increase our effectiveness and to ensure that our behavior is ethical.

Standards for Professional Practice

Generally stated, the ethical responsibilities of professors include, in the words of the American Association of University Professors (1987), "to seek and state the truth as they see it . . . [and to] encourage the free pursuit of learning in their students." Murray, Gillese, Lennon, Mercer, and Robinson (see Chapter Eight) have developed a list of ethical principles for university teaching that include maintaining competence, dealing openly with sensitive topics, contributing to student development, avoiding exploitation and discrimination, avoiding conflicts of interest, maintaining confidentiality in student communications, respecting the dignity of our colleagues, and ensuring valid and fair assessment of students.

Scriven (1981) states that ensuring that what we teach matches what was promised and ensuring that what we test matches what we teach are among the minimal ethical obligations of professors. Wilcox and Ebbs (1992) present their principles of ethical practice as guidelines: respect autonomy, do no harm, benefit others, be just and be faithful—a list that echoes the recommendations of Robinson and Moulton (1988). Svinicki (1994) translates principles for ethical practice into a set of questions that include "Am I acting in ways which respect freedom and treat others as autonomous? . . . Am I causing harm? . . . Do my actions benefit the other person rather than myself? . . . [and] What are the assumptions on which I base my actions and are they valid?" (p. 277).

Svinicki's last question suggests that each of us has a professional responsibility to examine our assumptions—the values and beliefs that inform our practice. Furthermore, we need to determine whether our actual practice is consistent with our values, beliefs, and principles and to try to reduce inconsistencies.

Gaps Between What We Say and What We Do

Most of us in college and university teaching proclaim our commitment to the standards and obligations mentioned in the previous section. We are concerned about being effective as teachers and scholars, and we are committed to learning—our students' learning and our own learning. We pride ourselves on our dedication to searching for truth. We see ourselves as effective problem solvers who are pledged to generating valid information about the important issues at hand—information that will form the basis for free and informed choices about which actions should be taken.

To what extent are our practices consistent with these values that we espouse? The concepts of the "reflective practitioner" and "theories of action" introduce and inform the process I propose for reflecting on this question of consistency and, more generally, on the ethics of our practice.

In *The Reflective Practitioner: How Professionals Think in Action*, Donald Schon (1983) describes how professionals behave when confronting problems, puzzles, or surprises—those difficult or ambiguous situations in our practice in which our usually skillful and automatic responses don't seem to be adequate. We first *frame*, or name, the problem. Next, we *take action* to solve the problem we have named, to explore the situation, or to test some hypothesis about the problematic situation. We then *listen to the "talk back"* from the situation, examining the consequences of our actions *to see if we have solved the problem we have named*. If we have, we move on. If not, we either *find new action strategies* or we *find a new name* for the problem—we *reframe* it. This process of framing, acting, and responding to the consequences of our actions Schon calls "reflection-in-action." Thus, as we deal with difficult situations we reflect *in* action. Our efforts to improve our practice require that we reflect *on* how we were thinking and acting.

Argyris and Schon (1974) have developed the concept of "theories of action." Essentially, they argue that we design our actions and that we have theories about how to design our actions in order to achieve our intentions. Thus, we have theories—perhaps only implicit—about how to confront a student, how to give constructive feedback, how to be helpful, encouraging, supportive, and so on.

Argyris and Schon (1974) distinguish between two types of theories of action. Our "espoused theories" are those rationales we give to ourselves and to others to explain our actions. Our "theories-in-use" are the rules we *actually* follow when we act. These latter rules—programs for action, as it were—are necessary for us to be able to manage in a complex world. They allow us to act automatically, quickly, and competently, often without much apparent thought. They allow us to maintain a satisfactory balance among the fundamental values that govern our actions but which can sometimes also be in conflict. For example, in the case sketched earlier, Professor C decides to ease in, in order to balance being caring and being honest with a student about the quality of her work, so that his feedback doesn't cause her further upset.

One purpose of reflecting on our actions, particularly in those difficult situations in our practice when we have not achieved our intentions, is to discover our theories-in-use, those rules that apparently were guiding our actions. If we are to change our behavior in order to become more effective, we first need to identify the rules we were following. We need to discover how we were thinking in order for our actions to make sense to us.

We also need to identify the gaps between what we espouse and what we do—between what we intend and what we produce. We need to discover these gaps and to identify any rules we may have been following that inadvertently led us to produce undesired or unintended consequences. Since no one would intentionally design actions to be ineffective, it follows that in some instances we may well be unaware of those rules. Thus, we must be concerned not only about those gaps between what we practice and what we preach—and in some cases, what we teach—but also about our unawareness.

Discovering Our Theories-in-Use

Our theories-in-use incorporate the values that govern our actions and the rules we use in choosing strategies to achieve our intentions. Professor C's governing values (help students, be caring, don't cause upset, and so on) led him to choose a strategy, easing in, in order to achieve his goal of helping the student. Our governing values influence the goals we set for ourselves, as well as the strategies we choose.

Since we can't always depend on what we *claim to do* (our espoused theories) to be an accurate reflection of what we *actually do*, Argyris and Schon (1974) suggest that we should write case studies about difficult episodes in our practice. They suggest a format for these case studies that includes actual dialogue (as well as we can recall it), together with any relevant thoughts and feelings we might have had that were not communicated during the conversation. Analysis of cases involves examining three principal areas: your action strategies, the consequences of those actions, and the values that underlie the strategies.

Identifying Action Strategies

Our actions and the strategies that inform them are always designed to solve the problems we have set for ourselves. This is the fundamental idea of reflection-in-action. Professor C's problem was how to help an upset student whose work had declined. Professor J set her problem as helping a student with an attitude whose work was deteriorating. If asked, these teachers probably would say they wanted to be caring and supportive, or direct and honest. By examining what was said and done to solve problems we try to infer what strategies seem actually to be operative.

After identifying the strategies, we need to assess them. Examining consequences is one means of doing this: did the outcomes of the strategies indicate success in achieving the intended goals? Did Professors C and J accomplish what they hoped to achieve?

Actions can also be assessed in terms of the extent to which they are consistent with promoting valid information about the problem at hand. Without valid information we are unlikely to be able to choose effective strategies to solve the problem we have set for ourselves (we may not even be able to discover if we have *named* the problem correctly). The following set of questions can be applied to analyzing any case study in order to identify behaviors that are counterproductive to effective problem solving.

- *Have I made attributions or evaluations that I did not illustrate or test?* For example, Professor C evaluated his student's work as deteriorating, but he did not provide illustrations to the student nor did he ask her if she agreed with his conclusion. He assumed she was under strain and fragile, but he did not check that out with her. Professor J explained her evaluation of her student's work (which she didn't illustrate or test) by attributing to him an attitude problem (which she also did not illustrate or test.)
- *Have I advocated actions without inviting inquiry?* For example, Professor J states what *she* would like to do ("talk about your future") without asking the student for his point of view.
- *Have I withheld relevant information?* For example, Professor C believes that his student is under strain and too fragile to handle his evaluation of her work, so he decides to be indirect in his approach. He does not tell her any of this. Professor J concludes that her previous approaches have been ineffective and that she must now change strategies and be "fairly honest" with her student. She withholds all of this thinking from him.

Assessing Consequences

What consequences might follow from the action strategies and resultant behaviors described in the previous section?

- *These strategies could lead to miscommunication, misunderstanding, and mistrust.* If I make assumptions about you and don't test them with you, yet act as if I am correct, I may be wrong. Thus, *I* will be the one responsible for limiting the generation of valid information necessary for effective problem solving. For example, Professor C's student may be fragile, but she may be able to handle C's feedback. Professor J's student may not agree about her assessment of the deterioration in his work or his attitude problem. He could easily decide that there is little point in discussing his future with a professor whose mind is already made up.
- *These strategies could be self-sealing.* Sometimes we can act in ways that protect our assumptions from any possibility of being disconfirmed—we "self-seal" them. For example, by not testing his view of his student as fragile, Professor C prevents himself from discovering the accuracy of his judgment. By not discussing her own assessment of her previous strategies, Professor J prevents herself from generating more complete information about their impact and how they might be improved.
- *They could be self-fulfilling.* Actions can also create the outcomes that were originally assumed to be true. For example, Professor J's direct and blunt behavior toward her student may lead him to believe that J has already made up her mind and is closed to any real discussion of the issues involved. He may respond by withdrawing or becoming belligerent; either action could be interpreted as proof that he has an attitude. Perhaps it is J's behavior toward the student that has caused the attitude, but J's behavior will prevent her from learning that.

Professor C asks a series of leading questions designed to lead the student to judge her own work as poor and to protect C from pronouncing his judgment and being the cause of her upset. By doing so, he may cause a student who already realizes that her work is slipping to conclude that her work must be horrible, since the professor is being so cautious. Paradoxically, his indirectness may produce the very result it was designed to avoid: cause the student to be upset. Her response could be interpreted as confirming his original judgment that she was fragile and wouldn't be able to handle the truth.

- *They could limit learning.* Action strategies might also limit the learning of both the professor and the student. It is unlikely that Professor C will learn whether or not his student is fragile, and whether she wants or needs his version of caring. The student is unlikely to learn what she is doing that the teacher perceives as fragile and that leads others to be reluctant to give her the honest feedback she may need to improve her performance, or to be cared about in a way that is truly helpful. Professor J is unlikely to learn how to be more effective with a student when her first strategy fails. The student is unlikely to learn more effective ways to deal with his attitude and his work.

- *They could lead to distancing and disconnection.* Strategies that are self-sealing or self-fulfilling might also lead people to be disconnected from their own reasoning. People may espouse a commitment to truth and learning, yet behave in ways that are counterproductive to achieving those goals. They may be distanced from their responsibility for creating the consequences they achieve and may blame others for undesired consequences.

Thus, we have the paradoxical situation in which Professors C and J, with the best of intentions to be helpful, caring, and honest, behave in ways that could lead to increased misunderstanding and to limiting the learning of both the professor and the student.

How do we account for such behavior? I now turn to an examination of the values that lead to these action strategies.

Uncovering Governing Values

Argyris and Schon (1974) argue that while most of us say we are caring and honest—we espouse our commitment to truth, to productive reasoning, to effective problem solving, and to learning—we often behave, as did Professors C and J, in ways that produce exactly opposite results. Withholding information, not illustrating or not testing attributions and evaluations, and advocating a position without inviting inquiry are three results of the following values: control the purpose of meetings; win, don't lose; avoid negative emotion; and be rational. Most of us are reluctant to acknowledge that values such as these may inform some of our actions.

Professor C would not be likely to describe himself as controlling; he thinks he is trying to be helpful. He wants to avoid contributing to the upset of one of his students because he cares. However, Professor C is also trying to control the meeting unilaterally by controlling the meanings he has attached to the student's work and to her behavior. He is trying to prevent her from getting upset and perhaps is trying to protect himself from having to deal with her distress. C is trying to save face for himself and for the student. With the best of intentions to be caring and helpful, C is behaving in ways that limit his effectiveness and that limit his own learning and that of his student. (Readers will recognize that each of these conclusions is an inference with which they may disagree and which certainly would have to be checked out with Professor C.)

Professor J is being direct and honest because she wants to help her student. However, she is also unilaterally controlling the meeting as well as the meanings she has attached to the student's behavior (it is deteriorating and he has an attitude) and to her own behavior (her previous efforts did not work, so now she should be honest).

Each of us can examine our own behavior, using our own case studies, and determine the underlying values. The important issue here is not control, but *unilateral* control and the consequences of these behaviors for effective problem solving and for learning.

Social Virtues

Most people, after examining their behavior using case studies from difficult situations in their practice, acknowledge—albeit with surprise and some reluctance—that there are gaps between what they say and what they do. But they wonder, "What else could I have done?" Surely it would be heartless and uncaring for Professor C to bluntly tell an upset student that her work has seriously deteriorated. It would have been dishonest for Professor J to withhold her thinking about her student's attitude and its impact on his work. Argyris (1985) challenges us to rethink the "social virtues." What are the meanings we attach to caring, support, honesty, respect, and integrity? What consequences flow from these meanings that might be counterproductive to effective problem solving and learning?

Even if Professor C is correct in his assumptions, could it be that his version of being helpful by trying to protect his student is not at all helpful to the student and perhaps even disrespectful? I believe it would have been more helpful to the student for Professor C to share with her the basis for his judgments, to illustrate what she was doing and saying, to present his reasoning, and to invite the student into dialogue. His reasoning and hers could be examined in this conversation. Respecting her would assume that she would be able to engage in this conversation, to examine her own behavior without losing her self-esteem or giving up her power to choose to stop. In short, it is probably patronizing for C to assume, without checking, that his student cannot handle his version of the truth and that he can and should help her by being indirect.

Integrity means more than sticking to a point of view in spite of opposition from others. It means both advocating your position and inviting inquiry—being open to learning and to having your conclusions disconfirmed. Honesty means more than telling others everything you think and feel. It means creating conditions where it is more likely that people can speak and hear without distortion.

It is not easy for us to change our behavior, to present our interpretations and to hear different points of view, and to combine advocacy with illustrations, inquiry, and tests. In one workshop (Smith and Schwartz, 1988), a professor who had been withholding her evaluation that one of her students was "scowling and attempting to test her authority" agreed that she should have confronted this student earlier in the course, before the situation got out of control. "The student would probably have denied it," she went on to say, "but at least I would have had the satisfaction [of not bottling it up]."

It is not enough to make your premises, reasoning, and conclusions public instead of withholding them. You also need to be open to really considering other explanations. The professor's describing as a denial an explanation that disagreed with her version of the truth suggests just how hard it can be to be truly open to inquiry and learning.

In summary, a careful examination of the way we reasoned and acted in difficult situations may reveal that we were acting in ways that are counterproductive to learning and effective problem solving; that our actions flowed from a set of values we did not espouse; and that definitions of caring, support, honesty, and the other social virtues led us to act in ways that were uncaring, dishonest, and unsupportive.

Creating a Better World: New Ways of Acting

Where might this process lead? What can we say and do that will combine advocacy and illustration with inquiry and testing in order to generate the valid information necessary to support free and informed choices? The following examples suggest what Professors C and J, were they to follow such a process, might say to their students. How effective do you think they would be?

Professor C might say to his student, "I would like to talk to you about some concerns I have about the quality of your recent work. However, I'm also concerned that this might not be a good time for you since you seem to be under some strain and somewhat fragile lately. [An illustration could be provided.] If I'm correct, then I'm in a bind. I want to help you by discussing your work, but I'm worried such a discussion might add to your upset and I don't want to do that. What do you think about what I've just said?"

Professor J might say, "I noticed a deterioration in your work recently [provides illustration]. I would like to know if you agree with my conclusion." [If the student agrees, they could go on to discuss the causes and possible remedies.]

Professor J might also say, "I want to help you be successful in this course, if that is what you want. I believe that if you continue to work at this level you might not pass because [provides illustration]. I'm concerned that my previous conversations with you haven't led to any improvement, and I'm not sure what else I can do. What do you think?"

She might continue, "I have noticed you doing (saying) [provides illustration]. This leads me to think you have a chip on your shoulder that is interfering with your work. Do you agree?"

The research of Argyris (1982) and Argyris, Putnam, and Smith (1985) suggests that this process of change is much harder than it seems. You may realize that you espouse values and behaviors (such as joint control or not withholding information) that you will find difficult to produce in real interactions. I would be withholding important information by not alerting you to these difficulties. Nevertheless, I believe that if you agree that your behavior is not up to the standards you desire and if you are not achieving the outcomes you intend, this analysis can provide a framework for professional growth and development that is well worth the effort.

References

American Association of University Professors. "Statement on Professional Ethics," *Academe,* 1974, 73 (4), 49.

Argyris, C. *Reasoning, Learning and Action: Individual and Organizational.* San Francisco: Jossey-Bass, 1982.

Argyris, C. *Strategy, Change and Defensive Routines.* New York: Harper Business, 1985.

Argyris, C. *Knowledge for Action: A Guide for Overcoming Barriers to Organizational Change.* San Francisco: Jossey-Bass, 1993.

Argyris, C., Putnam, R., and Smith, D. *Action Science.* San Francisco: Jossey-Bass, 1985.

Argyris, C., and Schon, D. A. *Theory in Practice: Increasing Professional Effectiveness.* San Francisco: Jossey-Bass, 1974.

Argyris, C., and Schon, D. A. *Organizational Learning.* Reading, Mass.: Addison-Wesley, 1978.

Robinson, G. M., and Moulton, J. *Ethical Problems in Higher Education.* Englewood Cliffs, N.J.: Prentice-Hall, 1985.

Schon, D. A. *The Reflective Practitioner: How Professionals Think in Action.* New York: Basic Books, 1983.

Schon, D. A. *Educating the Reflective Practitioner.* San Francisco: Jossey-Bass, 1987.

Scriven, M. "Summative Teacher Evaluation." In J. Millman (ed.), *Handbook of Teacher Evaluation.* Newbury Park, Calif.: Sage, 1981.

Smith, R. A., and Schwartz, F. "Improving Teaching by Reflecting on Practice." In J. Kurfiss, L. Hilsen, S. Kahn, M. D. Sorcinelli, and R. Tiberius (eds.), *To Improve the Academy: Resources for Student, Faculty, and Institutional Development,* Vol. 7. POD/New Forums Press, 1988.

Svinicki, M. "Ethics in College Teaching." In W. J. McKeachie, *Teaching Tips: Strategies, Research, and Theory for College and University Teachers* (9th ed.) Lexington, Mass.: Heath, 1994.

Wilcox, J. R., and Ebbs, S. L. *The Leadership Compass: Values and Ethics in Higher Education.* ASHE–ERIC Higher Education Report No. 1. Washington, D.C.: George Washington University, 1992.

RONALD A. SMITH, *a former professor of mathematics, is currently director of the Learning Development Office and professor of adult education at Concordia University, Montreal. He is a 3M Canada teaching fellow.*

Herein are practical suggestions on how colleges and universities can develop and carry out a variety of initiatives, particularly seminars and workshops, that can be directed toward enhancing engagement with ethical issues and promoting ethical behavior.

Toward More Ethical Teaching

Linc. Fisch

Ideally, all faculty members when they enter their very first classrooms would have a high degree of awareness of the ethical dimensions of teaching and understanding of the subtle complexities of ethical problems and issues. They would recognize the diverse perspectives that people bring to human interactions. They would recognize the values that inform their own behavior and the behavior of others, and they would know how to deal with situations when values are in conflict. They would have conscious commitment to ethical behavior. They would behave in ways that preclude ethical problems, and they would have the knowledge and skills to resolve problems that occur. And the campus climate would actively reinforce all this.

The reality is otherwise for many of us. We go about our teaching and other professional activities focused on other things—blocking out courses, composing and grading examinations, preparing for instruction (things that are important academic responsibilities, I'm bound to note)—rarely with even a passing thought given to the ethical dimensions of what we are doing. We often come to our understanding of ethics in our teaching only through observing a situation involving one of our colleagues or—worse yet—by suddenly and unexpectedly finding ourselves sinking into an ethical quagmire, not knowing what alligators may lurk therein. In such cases, experience is an especially hard teacher. And throughout most campuses, ethical teaching is a seldom-discussed topic, falling far behind funding, salaries, parking, and athletics.

I do not indict all faculty members, nor do I suggest that great numbers are totally uninformed about ethical issues. But I do think that far too many bring naiveté to the subject, at ultimate disservice to their students, their institution, and themselves. Neither do I indict all colleges and universities, but far too few have claim to giving strong consideration to these matters.

Some Colleges and Universities *Have* Undertaken Initiatives

Although some institutions may take a casual, passive approach to this important subject, not all do. Let me cite just a few notable exceptions. A number of colleges and universities in the United States and Canada have conducted workshops on ethics and values, using either resource persons from their campus or specially invited consultants. Indiana University of Pennsylvania held a Friday-Saturday workshop and invited representatives from nearby institutions to attend. Bucknell University held a pair of seminars on ethics in teaching, from which developed a continuing study group that reads and discusses novels and other writings dealing with ethics on campus (May Sarton's *The Small Room* was one). Slippery Rock University programmed a half-day ethics workshop for faculty and students into its fall professional day, then followed up with related articles in its periodic newsletter for faculty.

The University of Colorado at Boulder distributed to teaching assistants and others "Ethics and Traditions of Academia," a one-page broadside based on the AAUP's "Statement on Professional Ethics." Courses in a number of universities have used student performances or staged readings of A. R. Gurney's *Another Antigone* as a basis for extended discussions of the ethical issues in academia that the play raises.

Mansfield University annually schedules a global issues week. In 1994, when the focus was on ethics, education—with sessions for faculty and for faculty and students together—was included prominently along with the fields of business, medicine, and law. The University of Wisconsin System regularly schedules three-day seminars on ethics in teaching at the annual Faculty College attended by representatives from the system's units throughout the state. The president of Georgetown University devoted his opening address to faculty in 1994 to ethical reflection. At the 1995 national conference on the training and employment of teaching assistants (the faculty of the future), two sessions focused on ethics and values in teaching.

Essential Characteristics of Effective Initiatives

Of course, we cannot ensure ethical behavior in teaching just by generating—in isolation—convocations (however inspiring), articles (however stimulating), seminars (however dynamic), or statements of ethical principles (however valid), even though these elements can be useful initiators and reinforcers. In order to develop in faculty (individually and collectively) the awareness, understanding, perspectives, commitment, behavior that precludes problems, and skill in resolving problems that I suggest above, it is necessary for them to work with each other steadily and consistently in trying to deal with ethical issues and problems, whether real or hypothetical. Only through an honest and open exchange of ideas will faculty members be able to comprehend the many perspectives that may have validity in considering ethical issues. Only by testing ideas with each other will faculty members come to recognize, reconsider, and perhaps even refine their own positions—reaching new commitments or renewing those already held. Successful efforts require deliberately designed and coordinated goals and programs. Above all, they require full institutional support.

Discussion as a Method of Choice

In academic settings, when the objectives of instruction are affective—generating awareness and understanding, clarifying values, producing commitment, or affecting attitudes—the method of choice is discussion. Indeed, most of the examples given above involve seminars or workshops that heavily employ discussions. Thus, it is useful to turn to consideration of some of the key concerns in using this method—in particular, starting discussions, managing them, and concluding them.

Getting Underway: Triggering and Focusing Discussion. An all-too-common caricature of a discussion leader has a professor lecturing to a class for 40 minutes (perhaps having reached the end of that day's notes) and then suddenly and precipitously springing on students either an invitation to react to the mass of material or to raise any questions they have. At best, this tactic leads to one-to-one conversations between student and teacher. At worst, it results in a deafening silence almost intolerable to most teachers. Within seconds, either they themselves respond further (essentially precluding student thought and response) or they dismiss the class with one of academia's most over-used clichés, "Well, I guess that's it for today."

That such a caricature persists is due to misconceptions of what a true discussion really is or what, in its finer hours, it could be: an open interaction among participants that encourages examining and challenging ideas, drawing insofar as possible upon the resources of the group members and guided (some might say moderated, managed, mediated, or orchestrated) by the professor so as to ensure progress toward the projected outcomes. Whatever those outcomes are, the challenge for discussion leaders, novices and veterans alike, is to bring the activity to early focus, to stimulate the participants, and to engage them quickly in dialogue with each other.

Fortunately, there is an abundance of options for accomplishing this. Among them are specifically designed "trigger" films and videos, short clips from films and videos, audiotapes, music, and slide-tapes. For the technologically challenged, there are case studies. For the dramatically inclined, skits, case studies, and even one-act plays can be performed by students, not to mention staged debates in which protagonist and antagonist have at each other, soon drawing the audience into the fray. For the minimalists among us, there can be half a dozen storyboard-like transparencies projected serially while we read the accompanying text. And the truly simplistic can snip an appropriate photograph or cartoon from the newspaper, enlarge it on a photocopier, convert it to a transparency, project it along with three or four questions, and launch a discussion with a one-frame trigger in a matter of moments, at practically no cost.

A critical element in these methods of bringing sharp focus, stimulus, and engagement to discussions is brevity. Brevity requires that material be left out, forcing participants to speculate on the precipitating causes of problems, the historical precedents, and a multitude of other factors that mimic circumstances that we face in real life. As a result, they jump into the discussion, literally making themselves, their emotions, and their responses part of it. Furthermore, by being succinct in our discussion kickoff we allow maximum time for participant interaction, the essential aspect of the session. Guidelines for this brevity are not fixed, but many trigger films and videos are surprisingly short, in the range of one to four minutes. Often a discussion moderator can excerpt an appropriate short clip from a longer piece, if the circumstances warrant it. Many case studies, whether read by participants or played out, require considerably less than ten minutes.

It also helps if the triggering mechanism is drawn from actual events and uses dialogue therefrom. It helps if it is characterized by visual images and emotional quality—even down to the (judicious-cum-appropriate) use of four-letter words that might emerge in similar confrontations encountered in real settings.

Brevity, incompleteness, realism, imagery, and emotion serve well the designer of materials and exercises that can launch discussions effectively, but two other matters also require special attention: the opening and closing segments of the material. The closing segment, the more important of these, should be open-ended. It should occur at just the right moment and on just the right note for participants to be poised on the edges of their chairs, ready and eager to jump into interaction with others in the group.

The opening segment's primary function is to grab the attention of group members, particularly since the triggering mechanism may be rather short. Those who design triggers often determine the closing first, then back up only as far as necessary to place an opening that establishes the setting of the episode to be portrayed. Then they try to include as little as possible between opening and closing. This is a good formula for composing any materials that are designed to have impact.

In discussions, it is desirable to create an interactive mode quickly, with as little fanfare as possible. An introduction or a mini-lecture that precedes discussion can easily retard the process of interaction. The best advice is simple: lead off with a suitable triggering mechanism and jump directly into the activity. Often the participation level is increased, especially in larger groups, by beginning the discussion in subgroups where members are more comfortable with sharing ideas and have more opportunities to contribute. Posing key focal questions to the subgroups also helps participants engage the material.

While there is no denying the value of developing discussion-focusing materials aimed at particular circumstances on a particular campus, a substantial and ever-growing supply of films, videos, and print materials for initiating discussions on ethical issues and problems already exists. Most of these are accompanied by discussion guides and are distributed at modest cost. The list of currently available resources at the end of this chapter includes selected discussion-triggering items and similar materials.

Articles and professional papers can also provide a basis and background for seminars and workshops. Care should be taken to have group participants read them in advance, else precious discussion time in a session will be lost. The chapters in this volume and the material that authors have cited would be a good source of possibilities. If material is photocopied, permission to do so should of course be obtained from the copyright holder. Often this is a simple matter, if the purpose is educational.

In Midstream sans Paddle: Discussion Management. Those with even modest experience in conducting discussions know the great variance from one topic to another, from one group to another, and from one day to another. No two discussions are alike and no one set of procedures can fit all or even a few situations.

To be sure, careful attention must be given to the opening, as I've suggested implicitly and briefly above. But what then? What if the discussion gets off on a tangent? What if one or two persons monopolize the dialogue? What if a few don't participate at all? What if hostility surfaces? What if, what if, what if? Dozens of problems and questions can arise, and dozens of answers can be given—sometimes different answers to the same question. Because circumstances vary widely, answers vary widely, too.

Of course, there is *one* answer that applies to *every* question: "It all depends"—on the group, the context, the setting, the circumstances at hand, and many other factors. But the conscientious discussion leader cannot blow off the responsibility of striving for a successful discussion by giving this semi-facetious One Answer, even if undue complications prevail. Neither can one default by countering that most discussion situations have so many peculiarities that they can't all be anticipated and prepared for.

Good discussion leaders gain the know-how, confidence, and courage to meet this polymorphous challenge by drawing ideas from treatises on the discussion method (too numerous to list here, but readily available) and from their colleagues, often by observing them in action. Coupling that with reflection on their own experiences, they develop strategies and guidelines that can serve across a broad spectrum of circumstances. Below are several that comprise a compass I have found useful. They are especially relevant in discussions with peers, many of whose experience and training represent major resources for the group.

- Govern actions and interventions by an assessment of what seems to be most likely to promote growth and development of individuals and of the group as a whole.
- Try to generate a non-evaluative, non-threatening environment conducive to free and open discussion.
- Treat each member of the group with dignity and integrity.
- Offer to the group members as much responsibility as possible for carrying on the discussion.

- Try to promote a relevant personal experience for each group member.
- Exemplify the discussion behaviors (such as careful listening and avoidance of judgment) that are expected of the members.
- Use judicious initiating, clarifying, and leading questions (rather than authoritative statements or rhetorical questions) to guide the flow of the discussion toward its intended purposes and to enhance the value of the experience for members.

And in Closing . . . Some teachers panic unless they can navigate discussions to full consideration of all possible matters subsumed under the topic at hand, along with all the answers to all the possible questions found therein. But rarely is such closure possible, and often it's not desirable.

Discussions are dynamic entities, and many seem almost to have a life and spirit of their own. Topics originally assessed as tangential to the purposes of the session may emerge as highly important to participants. Not having "covered all the material" or not having arrived at the precise point intended for a discussion is not necessarily evidence of failure or even cause for alarm. Indeed, some of the best discussions are those that turn participants toward some route for resolution and send them on their way *still actively engaged* in the material, ready and eager to pursue it further on their own. Discussion leaders who accomplish these circumstances have done their jobs well.

To be sure, this state of suspended animation can be uncomfortable for both group members and leader. Although I do not condone another caricature of the discussion leader who proclaims, "We haven't come to any answers or resolutions, but we are the better for having considered the question," there is some truth embedded in the statement (as there usually is in a caricature). Often a significant value of discussion is the effect on the participant caused by meeting the challenge of the questions and by considering the perspectives of other participants, not to mention having developed clearer and more significant questions to be pursued.

The wise leader is one who does not leave these things to chance, but who actively works for them as the discussion is guided. And wise also is the leader who ensures at least some clarification of the questions, consideration of the options, and the beginnings of resolving issues and putting things into place in the minds of participants.

Knowledge of discussion principles, advance thought and preparation, and appropriate attitude are key factors in managing effective discussions about ethical issues. Discussions are often not as easy to conduct as lectures or other tightly controlled instructional formats. But they can be stimulating and can result in significant growth of the participants. Thus, they can be rewarding experiences for both the group members and the facilitator.

Additional Initiatives and Focal Questions

Examples earlier in this chapter suggested the breadth of possible initiatives conducted at system, university, college, division, and department levels and devoted to ethical issues: convocations, retreats, workshops, and seminars. New faculty members would be an especially appropriate target group. At any level faculty members can write and contribute case studies, based on their own experience, for consideration by their colleagues. Articles in faculty newsletters or distributed periodically can have an impact, though a relatively modest one compared to interactive initiatives.

There are also less structured opportunities for engaging ethical issues: ad hoc reading or study groups, luncheons involving clusters of faculty (or even just three or four informally gathered in the faculty dining room or lounge), pairs of faculty (whether or not linked through a mentoring program), and individual faculty members acting on their own. Although individual efforts can be quite useful, the opportunity to share and test ideas with others usually has a significant synergistic effect on outcomes.

For the faculty member who wishes to pursue the topic independently, the reflective process suggested by Ronald Smith in Chapter Eleven may be a good place to start. Below are examples of other exercises and focal questions that may be employed (responses in writing are often more productive than just thinking about a situation or a question). Most of these questions, largely drawn from chapters in this sourcebook, are also suitable for consideration by groups of colleagues.

- Consider your teaching performance in a recent class. What were the deeper values or "stakes" in what you presented and how you presented it? Examine this from the students' point of view as well as from your own.
- If students asked you, within the context of a class discussion, to reveal your political philosophy, religious affiliation, or sexual preference, how would you respond? Why?
- Are you always the dominant partner in the student-teacher relationship? Examine situations in which you could empower students to assume a dominant role to their educational advantage.
- Consider someone you think to be a "great teacher." What qualities do you admire in this person? How does this teacher exhibit an awareness of "what's at stake" in teaching? How has this person affected your own teaching?
- What are the values, virtues, and "habits of the heart" that you invoke (consciously or unconsciously) most often in your interactions with students?
- At what point (if ever) does the power to assign grades become "abuse of power" in faculty-student sexual relationships? What role does faculty power play in sexual harassment cases? How can the warning signs of such a situation be recognized?
- How do close friendships with students affect one's role as the teacher of an assigned course? What are the "up" sides and "down" sides of the issue? What are the limits?
- What are the advantages and disadvantages of faculty members' revealing their personal value systems or beliefs to students? Are there any discernible guidelines to assist in decision-making about self-revelations after self-reflection?

- What topics currently "hot" in your particular academic culture call for ethical judgments? What are the deep values embedded within these issues and situations?
- Explore issues chosen from the Timeless Questions section of Chapter Thirteen, such as, should there be a balance of power inside the classroom and outside?

The Journey Toward More Ethical Teaching

The ultimate goal of the endeavors of which I speak in this chapter is to help faculty members reach toward a higher sense of ethical teaching through critical reflection. No amount of indoctrination or laying on of hands or memoranda can speed them on this adventure. This is a personal quest that faculty members must undertake individually. And it's a quest that is never completed. To paraphrase John Dewey, it is not perfection, but the ever-enduring process of perfecting, maturing, and refining that is our aim.

As colleagues and institutional leaders, let us do all we can to help guide and support each other on this important journey.

Selected Resources and Sources, Briefly Annotated

The following is not a comprehensive list, but offers a variety of resources that may be useful for those wishing to undertake initiatives toward enhancing the climate for ethical teaching. Where sources might be relatively unknown to readers, sufficient information is given so that contact may be made.

Print Materials

Cahn, S. M. (ed.). *Morality, Responsibility, and the University.* Philadelphia: Temple University Press, 1990.

Dill, D. D. (ed.). "Ethics and the Academic Profession." *Journal of Higher Education,* 1982, *53,* (entire issue No.3).

Issues in Academic Ethics is a multivolume series edited by Steven M. Cahn and published by Rowman & Littlefield Publishers, Inc. (4720 Boston Way, Lanham, Md. 20706, telephone: 1–800–462–6420, fax: 301–459–2118). The first volumes were issued in 1994. Each volume is devoted to a central topic and typically consists of original text by the volume author combined with selected previously published writings relevant to the topic.

May, W. F. (ed.). *Ethics and Higher Education.* New York: Macmillan, 1990.

The reader also is referred to individual chapters in this sourcebook for other relevant writings cited by authors.

Case Studies

Keith-Spiegel, P., Wittig, A. F., Perkins, D. W., Balogh, D. W., and Whitley, B. E., Jr. *The Ethics of Teaching: A Casebook.* Muncie, Ind.: Ball State University, 1993.

Published by the BSU Department of Psychological Science (telephone: 317–285–1690), this book contains 165 cases, each typically a paragraph long and accompanied by a brief analysis.

Silverman, R. and Welty, W. M. *Case Studies for Faculty Development.* Pleasantville, N.Y.: Center for Case Studies in Education, Pace University.

The Center for Case Studies in Education can be reached by mail at 861 Bedford Road, Pleasantville, N.Y. 10570; by telephone at 914–773–3873; by fax at 914–773–3878; and by electronic mail at welty@pacevm.dac.pace.edu. This volume contains seventeen print cases, two to four pages each, with discussion guide.

Learning Research Ethics as a Community. WWW Ethics Center for Engineering and Science.

This material is available on the World Wide Web at http://web.mit.edu/ethics/www/. Interested persons also may call Carolyn Whitbeck at 617–258–1631, or may inquire by fax at 617–258–7018 or by e-mail at whitbeck@mit.edu. Currently, three topics are available, each consisting of readings, one or more scenarios, and a discussion guide.

Videotapes

With the exception of the Brigham Young University video, the following resources are series of short videos designed to trigger discussion about problem situations in teaching. The University of Kentucky series is the only one in which all of the episodes are oriented specifically to ethical issues, but several episodes in the other series focus on problems in teaching that have ethical overtones.

Integrity in Scientific Research: Five Video Vignettes. Washington, D.C.: American Association for the Advancement of Science, 1996.

Contact the AAAS by mail at 1333 H Street NW, Washington, D.C. 20005, by telephone at 202–326–6793, by fax at 202–289–4950, or by e-mail at afowler@aaas.org. Mark S. Frankel is the project director. This series consists of five videos, ranging in length from eight to ten minutes, together with a discussion and resource guide.

Toward an Ethical Learning Community. Provo, Utah: Brigham Young University, 1995.

This videotape may be obtained by writing the BYU Faculty Center, 167 HGB, Provo, Utah 84604–2710; by telephone at 801–378–5845; by fax at 801–378–5976; or by e-mail at louise_illes@byu.edu. Its running time is thirty-five minutes and it is accompanied by a discussion guide.

Race in the Classroom: A Multiplicity of Experience. Cambridge, Mass.: Harvard University, Derek Bok Center for Teaching and Learning, 1993.

This video is distributed by Anker Publishing Company, P.O. Box 249, Bolton, Mass. 01740–0249; telephone: 508–779–6190; fax: 508–779–6366. Orders can be placed with Publishers Business Services, Jaffrey, N.H. 03452–0390; telephone and fax: 603–532–7454. It consists of five vignettes with a total running time of 19 minutes, and includes a facilitator's handbook.

Dealing with Problems. Syracuse, N.Y.: Syracuse University, Center for Instructional Development, 1996.

This video is distributed by Anker Publishing Company, P.O. Box 249, Bolton, Mass. 01740–0249; telephone: 508–779–6190; fax: 508–779–6366. Orders can be placed with Publishers Business Services, Jaffrey, N.H. 03452–0390; telephone and fax: 603–532–7454. It consists of seventeen vignettes and has a total running time of 20 minutes; a discussion guide is included.

Critical Incidents; Critical Incidents II: Close Encounters of the Academic Kind; Critical Incidents III: Legends of the Fall Term, Victoria, B.C.: University of Victoria, 1993–1996.

These tapes are available from the UVic Learning & Teaching Centre, P.O. Box 3025, Victoria, B.C. V8W 3P2; or by telephone at 604–721–8571, by fax at 604–721–6494, or by e-mail at bjudson@uvvm.uvic.ca. Andy Farquharson is the project director. Each video in the series is composed of ten episodes and is accompanied by a discussion guide.

Trigger Films on College Teaching, Series E, Lexington, Ky.: University of Kentucky, 1993.

These videotapes are available from the Office of Media Production and Design, 170 Taylor Ed Building, University of Kentucky, Lexington, Ky. 40506; telephone: 606–257–8474; fax: 606–323–1927. Linc. Fisch is the project director. Five episodes are currently available, running from two to seven minutes each. The films are accompanied by a discussion guide.

Associations and Conferences

The Association for Practical and Professional Ethics (410 North Park Avenue, Bloomington, Ind. 47405; telephone: 812–855–6450; fax: 812–855–3315; e-mail: appe@ucs.indiana.edu; direct inquiries to the attention of Brian Schrag, executive secretary). APPE usually holds conferences in March and in midsummer.

The Society for Values in Higher Education (c/o Georgetown University, Box 57–1205, Washington, D.C. 20057; telephone: 202–687–3653; fax: 202–687–5094; e-mail: svhe@guvm.ccf.georgetown.edu; direct inquiries to the attention of Kathleen McGrory, executive director) usually holds its annual conference in late summer.

The American Association for Higher Education and Pace University's Center for Case Studies in Education cooperatively sponsor each summer an annual conference: "Using Cases for Reflective Teaching and Learning." Contact the Center for Case Studies in Education at Pace University, 861 Bedford Road, Pleasantville, N.Y. 10570; telephone, 914–773–3873; fax: 914–773–3878; e-mail: welty@pacevm.dac.pace.edu. Direct inquiries to the attention of William M. Welty, co-director.

LINC. FISCH held teaching appointments (mathematics, college teaching, community dentistry, and public health), as well as administrative and program development assignments, in several colleges and universities in Ohio, Michigan, and Kentucky for more than thirty-five years. He lives in Lexington, Kentucky, and is actively retired.

The daily lives of faculty are fraught with demands to make choices among options that often call for "deep value" decision making. Because of the unique relatedness of students and teachers, faculty ethical decision making can be both a private act and a public act of far-reaching consequence.

Ethics in Teaching: Putting It Together

Kathleen McGrory

> Bit by bit. Putting it together . . . piece by piece . . . Ev'ry moment makes a contribution, Ev'ry little detail plays a part . . . First of all, you need a good foundation . . . Takes a lot of earnest conversation—But without the proper preparation—Having just the vision's no solution—Ev'rything depends on execution . . . Ev'ry minor detail is a major decision. Have to keep things in scale, have to hold to your vision . . . Ev'ry word, ev'ry line, ev'ry glance, ev'ry movement you improve and refine. Then refine each improvement . . . Bit by bit. Putting it together, piece by piece . . . Putting it together— That's what counts.
>
> —Stephen Sondheim (*Sunday in the Park with George*)

This is a book about teaching, from the point of view of college and university faculty as ethical decision makers. The necessity to make moral, ethical, and even legal decisions in the daily course of our teaching careers—not merely to theorize about them or to teach ethics and decision making as academic disciplines—is what defines the ethical dimensions of college and university teaching, a neglected area in American graduate preparation for college teaching and in institutional efforts to enhance the quality of teaching practice.

Philosopher Elizabeth Minnich (1994) argues that the first question faculty need to ask themselves when faced with ethical decisions such as whether or not to share their political convictions with students is, "What's at stake?"— a way of framing the dilemma in terms of consequences before responding to the immediacy of the demand to act. The essays in this volume provide a range of answers to that question in regard to college teaching. As several of the authors make clear, citing arguments within the profession from Plato and Aristotle to Buber, Niebuhr, and Rawls, what is at stake in the ethical pursuit of good practice in teaching is nothing less than the soul and self of both student and teacher. At stake, too, is the moral well being of public life.

NEW DIRECTIONS FOR TEACHING AND LEARNING, no. 66, Summer 1996   © Jossey-Bass Publishers

Timeless Questions, Timely Answers

There is an urgency to find new solutions to old questions that, despite the antiquity of their original asking, have not yet been adequately answered for the post-nuclear, democratic, technological society that is right here, right now, in American colleges and universities.

- What *is* the ethical nature of the relationship of teacher to student?
- Is this a relationship that social analysts such as The Harvard Graduate School of Education's Charles Vert Willie (1981) would call "pathological," because one party is always dominant and one always sub-dominant?
- Is there security enough within the teacher-student relationship for the teacher to shed the role of authority and assume that of a learner among learners (David Smith in Chapter One, echoing Tom and Freire)?
- What conditions must pertain in order for this to happen? Is the teacher-student relationship necessarily one of equality or of inequality (D. Smith, Burgan, Baker, Rodabaugh, and R. Smith)?
- Are there ways of breaking out of binary imperatives to explore options in between without changing irrevocably the balance of power in the classroom?
- Should there be a balance of power in the classroom and outside (Hanson; Murray and associates)?

A department chair in a state university learned firsthand about the role of faculty in affecting students' "developmental identities" (Burgan) and about power issues that can be testing grounds for faculty judgment about relationships. A Vietnam veteran one day came to her to "unload" his disenchantment with an introductory philosophy course in which his professor (the subject was ethics) appeared not to respect his students, yet insisted they call him by his first name. The student's comment was instructive: "Great. We get to call him Andy and he gets to call us stupid."

Some of the suggestions offered in this sourcebook would work in any setting in which teaching and learning take place. Others require the special set of circumstances that pertain to higher education. All of them focus on the unique responsibility of the college teacher to be a reflective, ethical person, even in radically changing academic environments (Astin, 1993). No one should be much surprised that these diverse chapters about the same topic, ethical teaching, are remarkable for their unanimity on general principles and their diversity on specific applications to situations of ethical complexity.

Nearly every essay lists some key academic "deep values" (Reynolds in Chapter Nine, citing Niebuhr and Weber) that can serve as the ground of defensible public rationales for a faculty ethics of responsibility (Schwehn, 1992): honesty (D. Smith, Murray and associates, Reynolds); promise-keeping (D. Smith); fairness (D. Smith, Rodabaugh, Ray); competence (Murray and associates, Burgan); critical engagement with ideas, sensitivity, reflection (Hanson, Murray and associates); and respect (D. Smith, Reynolds). What constitutes a "sensitive topic" that might, in anyone's class, require the faculty member to invoke his or her own deep values for a command performance in discernment, fitting response, and (ultimately) moral choice (Reynolds)? For some, the triggering mechanism might be analysis of John Donne's poetry (Murray and associates); for others, creationism (Hanson), morality (Ray), mental illness (Burgan), homosexuality (Hanson), or student "attitudes" (R. Smith).

One concern looms large in any consideration of ethical teaching: the "fittingness" of faculty-student friendships outside the classroom (D. Smith, Baker, Rodabaugh, Murray and associates). What forms might these friendships ethically take, considering their impact on the educational role of the teacher? Possible responses are Buber's *precluded mutuality* (D. Smith); a *"mediated intimacy"* between student and teacher with subject-fields as both medium and barrier to abuse of power (Baker); a reminder of *the dangers to the developing identity* of the vulnerable student (Burgan); absolute *prohibition of "dual" relationships* (Murray and associates, R. Smith, AAUP 1974); and demonstration of *the inadequacy of current definitions of "ethical," "moral," and "legal"* to deter academic behaviors that might fall within the law but still violate the rights of students (Ray).

Another practical consideration is the degree to which self-revelation and advocacy are appropriate within the classroom (Hanson, R. Smith, Murray and associates). These essays, like life, suggest the impossibility of any statement of principles' offering unambiguous moral guidance (Reynolds). They offer, instead, differing values-based solutions to a variety of specific problems typically encountered by faculty today. Despite the various perspectives (each perhaps calling for different applications of personal values to the task of problem solving), all aim to achieve the same end: ethical teaching. These essays are obviously the start, not the finish, of what Jacques Barzun would have called a "long conversation" on ethical responsibilities of faculty.

Ethical Teaching as Community Activity

Faculty members need to discuss their own ethical solutions and academic procedures with peers and students. Departments and administrators should encourage ethical self-reflection in community (Fisch). The serious neglect of peer review in academia (Menges, 1991) has not only deprived faculty of opportunities for self-reflection but has also deprived them of occasions to act as peers in supporting or critiquing one another's ethical judgments (Keith-Spiegel and associates). Exercises of communal responsibility are even more salutary when these judgments occur within the framework of community concerns (academic or civic) and departmental discussions of ethical good practice.

There obviously is a need to institutionalize expectations of ethical behavior in teaching (Reynolds, Rodabaugh, Murray and associates, Ray) by more than formulated codes of ethics and laws (Rodabaugh, Murray and associates, Reynolds, Ray). Only with the participation of faculty as colleagues and institutional leaders in efforts to build more humane structures will institutions as moral entities arrive at genuine consensus on shared institutional values in theory and practice (Long, 1992). Only when faculty ethically engage with others will democratically structured environments model what they preach to students and the public at large (D. Smith, Hanson, Rodabaugh, Murray and associates, Reynolds, Ray, R. Smith)—namely, that ethical reflection leads to effective action. Several chapters here suggest a fruitful topic, appropriate to a variety of disciplines, for further discussion by faculty and students: if fairness were the organizing principle of institutions and classroom management, would one outcome for students be commitment to a just social order?

Faculty in the diverse world of American higher education cannot always count on public institutional support and peer affirmation for the ethical choices they must make in relative isolation. According to institutional mission statements and faculty senate proclamations, high ethical standards are the order of the day. Yet we know this is not universally true, and *that* is the compelling reason for this volume.

Private Virtue, Public Statement: Faculty as Logo

The pages of this sourcebook reveal several major areas of agreement about ethical behaviors that have long histories and traditional acceptance in the profession. But what of the role of the teacher as private person, as autonomous professional operating within the safe enclosure of academic freedom and all that this portends of privilege and responsibility? Teaching as a private act is dead. Once-private academic decisions now invite public scrutiny. The writing of a syllabus, seen here as a covenant with the larger community (Hanson) or the invitation to a student conference (R. Smith), can be the start of a chain of events that soon pass out of the faculty member's control. Contrary to most administrative textbook explanations, it is faculty members, not presidents, who stand as institutional "logo" in the eyes of students and the several "publics"—parents, siblings, alumni, donors—who have a stake in their education.

For all our postmodern disavowal of binary thinking as the only mode of analysis in cultural theory, philosophy, and social history, the essays in this volume reveal that the world in which the academic person lives and moves and acts has become increasingly bipolar, with the middle options disappearing. Institutions experience a similar decline in options to make moral and ethical choices about policies once taken for granted—for example, need-blind admissions, financial aid, and ethical sources of research funding. These economic and ethical losses follow hard on the heels of public criticism of the escalating costs of higher education and demands by students, parents, and employers to make teaching and higher learning more relevant to careers.

Mandates to do more with less are passed from voters to legislators to administrators to faculty. Claimants vie for priority among professorial allegiances to the profession, to the discipline, or to risky (in terms of rewards) interdisciplinary collaborations and community service. Responding to demands for ethnic, national, religious, and political correctness generates new imperatives in curricular choices.

Sometimes without regard for personal convictions of faculty members, departmental and institutional leaders often expect curricular choices to reflect unanimity. Today's faculty in many disciplines are stressed by invitations and incitements to take sides in the argument that a canon of some authoritative clout must be the controlling idea of the curriculum.

Amidst all the ferment and uncertainty of modern faculty roles and responsibilities (to some extent reflected in the chapters of this volume), one mediating principle emerges: *the professor's primary responsibility to students is directly related to the professor's understanding of his or her ethical self.* Its corollary: *the first step toward establishing faculty ethical identity within the ethos of higher education is self-reflection.*

Sic et Non

Evident in these pages are some problematic bipolarities of faculty roles, exposing myriad divisions and alliances within the larger faculty culture. Among the prevailing polarities that influence faculty response to ethical dilemmas are the tenured and the untenured, the teacher and the researcher, the activist and the contemplative, the traditionalist and the innovator, the junior faculty and the senior faculty, and the young and the old. It is particularly difficult to distinguish between young and old in the absence of tenure, unless a taste for MTV and postmodernism rather than age are decisive cultural markers.

Much of the faculty's everyday life occurs not in polar oppositions but in "the space between." Similarly, when ethical decisions must be made in the gray areas between moral or common sense and rule of law, individual faculty must rely on the same inner resources (whether or not buttressed by peer support and administrative reward): *informed individual conscience* and *one's own systems of personal and professional values.* In this respect, faculty differ little from their fellow men and women in the larger society, although their profession places them more often in direct power-potential relationships with students. It is this proximity that generates the need for frequent exercise of ethical judgment regarding the well being of students who come within their sphere of influence. This is an arena in which the rules of engagement are not always clear (Fisch, 1992), either to teachers, to students, or to the institution. These chapters provide an agenda for community consideration of those gray areas of ethical teaching and suggest resources for doing so.

Ethical Timeout

A basic premise of this volume is that the quality of faculty moral decision making can be improved by increased self-awareness and sensitivity to the rights of students, and by doing some "homework." The chapters in this volume invite faculty to declare an ethical timeout, to make a considered effort toward self-reflection, and to study and reflect on models of ethical behavior—even, perhaps, classical *Nomos* (Scott, 1995).

Timing is all. The time for serious ethical reflection is in advance of the necessity to make difficult decisions requiring a certain facility in doing "the right thing," to develop strengths in the practice of ethical behavior—what Aquinas and Bennett (1995) would call "virtues" and what Bellah (1985) called "habits of the heart."

Like the body, the "muscles" required for ethical response need exercise and nurture. Essential for the latter is a supportive framework of peers to help with ethical decision making about the issues that inevitably arise in teaching. Ethical exercise occurs within this conducive environment by reading about and carefully studying others' experiences of ethical dilemmas in the classroom and by inviting imaginative self-testing on ethical issues by means of case studies (Fisch).

Three of the chapters in this volume call upon faculty to use their *imagination* to ponder the ethical responsibilities of the teacher and to consider the consequences of committing to the highest-stakes game of all, the moral enterprise of teaching. Several authors consider the unique interpersonal relationship that Mary Burgan calls the "complicated minuet of generations"—a complex dance that requires striking a balance between rules and moral intuitions, excessive self-disclosure and excessive reserve, yet demands some of both. Others write about "what's at stake" in engaging the profession: nothing less than the soul or self, the moral identity and development of students whose minds we touch—or leave untouched—at our peril.

Mastery, Knowledge, and Power

Metaphors of "mastery" and "subject" naturally appear in ethically nuanced guises in any discussion of teaching and are suggestive of insights to be found in this volume. Novice teachers aspire to be master teachers, yet the graduate preparation of teachers does not often highlight for novices the ethical dimensions of mastery within the profession. The first ethical testing ground of new faculty is often the introductory course, a teaching task for which the latter years of graduate study hardly prepare the beginning teacher. Teachers new to the profession are sometimes surprised by outcomes of relational situations in which they saw no ethical land mines—for example, allegations of sexual harassment growing out of seemingly innocent exchanges of language with a student, or charges of discrimination, favoritism, or racism resulting from offers to help. Someone should have reminded us all, in graduate school, that knowledge is power—just as a wise graduate instructor at Columbia used to remind his students, "Never overlook the importance of the obvious."

Teachers have the power of the keys to knowledge, to career references, and to grade point averages. Students hunger for mastery, as much a form of control over their own futures as over the subjects we teach. Teachers have mastery, by virtue of their educational advantage. With so much potential for good or harm, the teacher who is unaware of his or her own power is a danger to society, particularly when the teacher as *transmitter* or *authority* enters the fragile culture of beginning undergraduate students.

Whether the teacher is seen as sole transmitter of knowledge, as moral equal, or as co-investigator, mastery of the requisite knowledge for the level of instruction assigned creates in and of itself a moral power base that is inescapable. To use this power for the good of the student, to transfer power to students through sharing knowledge and inducing learning, is the central moral imperative that emerges from this discussion of the transforming power of the ethical teacher.

Faculty or administrators might ignore the implications of the professional teacher's place within the power structure of the institution. They might fail to help faculty become self-reflective in community, or they might look the other way in instances of faculty abuse of power. But to do so is to invite comparison with the arrogant mastery by a god of the human Leda ("Did she put on his knowledge with his power?") in William Butler Yeats's (1928) mythic poem.

The glory of the human is still the ability to make moral choices. Ethical teaching requires transformation of structures and attitudes as well as persons if the promise of American higher education is to be realized. The chapters of this volume are a significant contribution toward realizing that promise.

References

American Association of University Professors. "Statement on Professional Ethics." *Academe,* 1974, 73 (4), 49.

Astin, A. W. *What Matters in College? Four Critical Years Revisited.* San Francisco: Jossey-Bass, 1993.

Bellah, R. N., Madsen, R., Sullivan, W. M., Swidler, A, and Tipton, S. M. *Habits of the Heart: Individualism and Commitment in American Life.* New York: Harper and Row, 1985.

Bennett, W. J. *The Book of Virtues.* New York: Simon & Schuster, 1993.

Fisch, L. "Power in College Teaching." *Teaching Excellence,* 1992, 4 (1).

Long, E. L., Jr. *Higher Education as a Moral Enterprise.* Washington, D.C.: Georgetown University Press, 1992.

Menges, R. J. "The Real World of Teaching Improvement: A Faculty Perspective." In M. Theall and J. Franklin (eds.), *Effective Practices for Improving Teaching.* New Directions for Teaching and Learning, no. 48. San Francisco: Jossey-Bass, 1991.

Minnich, E. K. *What Is at Stake? Risking the Pleasures of Politics.* Washington, D.C.: Society for Values in Higher Education, 1994 (Annual Fellows Lecture Monograph Series, 1996.)

Schwehn, M. R. *Exiles from Eden: Religion and the Academic Vocation.* New York: Oxford University Press, 1992.

Scott, J. B. "Sophistic Ethics in the Technical Writing Classroom: Teaching *Nomos.*" *Technical Communication Quarterly,* 1995, 14.2, 187–199.

Willie, C. V. *The Ivory and Ebony Towers: Race Relations and Higher Education.* Lexington, Mass.: Lexington Books, 1981.

Yeats, W. B. "Leda and the Swan." *Selected Poems and Two Plays of William Butler Yeats.* New York: Macmillan/Collier Books, 1970, p. 114.

KATHLEEN MCGRORY *is executive director of the Society for Values in Higher Education (Washington, D.C.) and former president of Hartford College for Women.*

INDEX

Academic ethics. *See* Ethics, academic

Academic Principles of Responsibility: and discerning judgment, 68–69; example of application of, 71–73; list of, 66–67; and principles of justice, 70

Academy. *See* Teaching

Action strategies: assessing consequences of, 84–85; identifying, 83

Adams, J. S., 38, 44

Administrators: and institutional fairness, 38, 43–44; and support of teachers, 43

Adolescence: and mastery, 19; and subjectivity, 17–20

Advocacy by teachers, ethics and, 33–36

Agape, 12

American Association of University Professors, 80, 88, 90, 103, 107

American Psychological Association, 63

Another Antigone, 90

Argyris, 82, 85, 87, 88

Aristotle, 26–27, 28, 32

Assessment: of students, valid, 62–63; types of, 67

Astin, A. W., 102, 107

Asymmetry, necessity of, 10

Attendance, fairness and, 41

Baker, R. L., Jr., 25

Balogh, D. W., 75, 97

Baron, R. M., 37, 45

Bell Jar, The, 22, 23

Bellah, R. N., 106, 107

Bennett, W. J., 106, 107

Bies, R. J., 38, 40, 41, 45

Bloom, A., 5–6, 14

Buber, 6, 9–10, 14

Bucknell University, 90

Burgan, M., 15, 16, 23, 102

Burns, J. M., 6, 8–9, 14

Cahn, S. M., 25–26, 32, 96

Cheating, 41, 77

Clark, D. J., 42, 45

Closing of the American Mind, The, 5–6, 14

Code of Ethics for Academic Staff, 63

Colleagues: and ethics initiatives, 95; intervening with, 75–78; respect for, 61–62; as teammates, 76, 77

College teaching: and ethical initiatives, 90–91, 94–96; ethical principles for, 57–63; implications of developmental stages for, 18–21, 102; institutional commitment to fairness in, 37–44; and public scrutiny of colleges, 104–105

Confidentiality, 61

Content competence, 58

Corkran, L., 41, 45

Day-to-day ethical issues, 11–13

Dealing with sensitive topics, 59

DeMore, S. W., 37, 45

Developmental identities in teaching: implications for college teaching, 18–21; and student-teacher relationships, 102; stages, students and, 16–18

Dill, D. D., 96

Discussion: focusing, 91–93; management of, 93–94; triggering, 91–93

Dispute resolution, fairness and, 44

Dual relationships between students and teachers, 60–61. *See also* Friendship; Student-teacher relationships

Ebbs, S. L., 81, 88

Encyclopedia of Ethics, 26, 32

Erikson, E. H., 16–19, 23

"Espoused theories," 82

Ethical decisions, 65–73

Ethical Investor, 13, 14

Ethical issues, day-to-day, 11–13

Ethical obligations: basic, 10–11; broader, 13–14; causal responsibility, 13; responsibility of last resort, 14; responsibility of proximity, 13–14; role responsibility, 13

Ethical principles: confidentiality, 61; content competence, 58; dealing with sensitive topics, 59; of dual relationships between students and teachers, 60–61; pedagogical competence, 58–59; respect for colleagues, 61–62; respect for institution, 63; student development, 59–60, 102; valid assessment of students, 62–63. *See also* Academic Principles of Responsibility

Ethical Principles in University Teaching, 57

Ethical reflection, modeling of, 35–36

ORDERING INFORMATION

NEW DIRECTIONS FOR EVALUATION is a series of paperback books that presents ideas and techniques for improving college teaching, based both on the practical expertise of seasoned instructors and on the latest research findings of educational and psychological researchers. Books in the series are published quarterly in spring, summer, fall, and winter and are available for purchase by subscription as well as by single copy.

SUBSCRIPTIONS for 1996 cost $50.00 for individuals (a savings of 35 percent over single-copy prices) and $72.00 for institutions, agencies, and libraries. Please do not send institutional checks for personal subscriptions. Standing orders are accepted. (For subscriptions outside of North America, add $7.00 for shipping via surface mail or $25.00 for air mail. Orders *must be prepaid* in U.S. dollars by check drawn on a U.S. bank or charged to VISA, MasterCard, or American Express.)

SINGLE COPIES cost $19.00 plus shipping (see below) when payment accompanies order. California, New Jersey, New York, and Washington, D.C., residents please include appropriate sales tax. Canadian residents add GST and any local taxes. Billed orders will be charged shipping and handling. No billed shipments to post office boxes. (Orders from outside North America *must be prepaid* in U.S. dollars by check drawn on a U.S. bank or charged to VISA, MasterCard, or American Express.)

SHIPPING (SINGLE COPIES ONLY): $10.00 and under, add $2.50; to $20.00, add $3.50; to $50.00, add $4.50; to $75.00, add $5.50; to $100.00, add $6.50; to $150.00, add $7.50; over $150.00, add $8.50.

DISCOUNTS FOR QUANTITY ORDERS are available. Please write to the address below for information.

ALL ORDERS must include either the name of an individual or an official purchase order number. Please submit your order as follows:
   Subscriptions: specify series and year subscription is to begin
   Single copies: include individual title code (such as TL54)

MAIL ALL ORDERS TO:
   Jossey-Bass Publishers
   350 Sansome Street
   San Francisco, CA 94104-1342

FOR SUBSCRIPTION SALES OUTSIDE OF THE UNITED STATES, CONTACT:
   any international subscription agency or Jossey-Bass directly.